Harvard
Business
Review

ON

CHANGE

THE HARVARD BUSINESS REVIEW PAPERBACK SERIES

The series is designed to bring today's managers and professionals the fundamental information they need to stay competitive in a fast-moving world. From the preeminent thinkers whose work has defined an entire field to the rising stars who will redefine the way we think about business, here are the leading minds and landmark ideas that have established the *Harvard Business Review* as required reading for ambitious businesspeople in organizations around the globe.

Other books in the series:

Harvard Business Review on Knowledge Management

Harvard Business Review on Leadership

Harvard Business Review on Measuring Corporate Performance

Harvard Business Review on Strategies for Growth

Harvard Business Review

ON

CHANGE

A HARVARD BUSINESS REVIEW PAPERBACK

The *Harvard Business Review* articles in this collection are available as individual reprints. Discounts apply to quantity purchases. For information and ordering, please contact Customer Service, Harvard Business School Publishing, Boston, MA 02163. Telephone: (617) 783-7500 or (800) 988-0886, 8 A.M. to 6 P.M. Eastern Time, Monday through Friday. Fax: (617) 783-7555, 24 hours a day. E-mail: custserv@hbsp.harvard.edu.

The paper used in this publication meets the requirements of the American National Standard for Permanence of Paper for Printed Library Materials Z39.49-1984.

Contents

Harvard Business Review

ON

CHANGE

Leading Change

Why Transformation Efforts Fail

JOHN P. KOTTER

Executive Summary

IN THE PAST DECADE, the author has watched more
than 100 companies try to remake themselves into better competitors. Their efforts have gone under many banners: total quality management, reengineering, right sizing, restructuring, cultural change, and turnarounds. In
almost every case, the goal has been the same: to cope
with a new, more challenging market by changing how
business is conducted.

A few of those efforts have been very successful. A
few have been utter failures. Most fall somewhere in
between, with a distinct tilt toward the lower end of the
scale. The lessons that can be learned will be relevant
to more and more organizations as the business environment becomes increasingly competitive in the coming
decade.

One lesson is that change involves numerous phases that, together, usually take a long time. Skipping steps creates only an illusion of speed and never produces a satisfying result. A second lesson is that critical mistakes in any of the phases can have a devastating impact, slowing momentum and negating previous gains. Kotter's lessons are instructive, for even the most capable managers often make at least one big error.

Over the past decade, I have watched more than 100 companies try to remake themselves into significantly better competitors. They have included large organizations (Ford) and small ones (Landmark Communications), companies based in the United States (General Motors) and elsewhere (British Airways), corporations that were on their knees (Eastern Airlines), and companies that were earning good money (Bristol-Myers Squibb). These efforts have gone under many banners: total quality management, reengineering, right sizing, restructuring, cultural change, and turnaround. But, in almost every case, the basic goal has been the same: to make fundamental changes in how business is conducted in order to help cope with a new, more challenging market environment.

A few of these corporate change efforts have been very successful. A few have been utter failures. Most fall somewhere in between, with a distinct tilt toward the lower end of the scale. The lessons that can be drawn are interesting and will probably be relevant to even more organizations in the increasingly competitive business environment of the coming decade.

The most general lesson to be learned from the more successful cases is that the change process goes through a series of phases that, in total, usually require a considerable length of time. Skipping steps creates only the illusion of speed and never produces a satisfying result. A second very general lesson is that critical mistakes in any of the phases can have a devastating impact, slowing momentum and negating hard-won gains. Perhaps because we have relatively little experience in renewing organizations, even very capable people often make at least one big error.

Error #1: Not Establishing a Great Enough Sense of Urgency

Most successful change efforts begin when some individuals or some groups start to look hard at a company's competitive situation, market position, technological trends, and financial performance. They focus on the potential revenue drop when an important patent expires, the five-year trend in declining margins in a core business, or an emerging market that everyone seems to be ignoring. They then find ways to communicate this information broadly and dramatically, especially with respect to crises, potential crises, or great opportunities that are very timely. This first step is essential because just getting a transformation program started requires the aggressive cooperation of many individuals. Without motivation, people won't help and the effort goes nowhere.

Compared with other steps in the change process, phase one can sound easy. It is not. Well over 50% of the companies I have watched fail in this first phase. What are the reasons for that failure? Sometimes executives underestimate how hard it can be to drive people out of their comfort zones. Sometimes they grossly overestimate how successful they have already been in increasing urgency. Sometimes they lack patience: "Enough with the preliminaries; let's get on with it." In many cases, executives become paralyzed by the downside possibilities. They worry that employees with seniority will become defensive, that morale will drop, that events will spin out of control, that short-term business results will be jeopardized, that the stock will sink, and that they will be blamed for creating a crisis.

A paralyzed senior management often comes from having too many managers and not enough leaders. Management's mandate is to minimize risk and to keep the current system operating. Change, by definition, requires creating a new system, which in turn always demands leadership. Phase one in a renewal process typically goes nowhere until enough real leaders are promoted or hired into senior-level jobs.

Transformations often begin, and begin well, when an organization has a new head who is a good leader and who sees the need for a major change. If the renewal target is the entire company, the CEO is key. If change is needed in a division, the division general manager is key. When these individuals are not new leaders, great leaders, or change champions, phase one can be a huge challenge.

Bad business results are both a blessing and a curse in the first phase. On the positive side, losing money does catch people's attention. But it also gives less maneuvering room. With good business results, the opposite is true: convincing people of the need for change is much harder, but you have more resources to help make changes.

But whether the starting point is good performance or bad, in the more successful cases I have witnessed, an individual or a group always facilitates a frank discussion of potentially unpleasant facts: about new competition, shrinking margins, decreasing market share, flat earnings, a lack of revenue growth, or other relevant indices of a declining competitive position. Because there seems to be an almost universal human tendency to shoot the bearer of bad news, especially if the head of the organization is not a change champion, executives in these companies often rely on outsiders to bring unwanted information. Wall Street analysts, customers, and consultants can all be helpful in this regard. The purpose of all this activity, in the words of one former CEO of a large European company, is "to make the status quo seem more dangerous than launching into the unknown."

One chief executive officer deliberately engineered the largest accounting loss in the history of the company.

In a few of the most successful cases, a group has manufactured a crisis. One CEO deliberately engineered the largest accounting loss in the company's history, creating huge pressures from Wall Street in the process. One division president commissioned first-ever customer-satisfaction surveys, knowing full well that the results would be terrible. He then made these findings public. On the surface, such moves can look unduly risky. But there is also risk in playing it too safe: when the urgency rate is not pumped up enough, the transformation process cannot succeed and the long-term future of the organization is put in jeopardy.

When is the urgency rate high enough? From what I have seen, the answer is when about 75% of a company's management is honestly convinced that business-as-usual is totally unacceptable. Anything less can produce very serious problems later on in the process.

Error #2: Not Creating a Powerful Enough Guiding Coalition

Major renewal programs often start with just one or two people. In cases of successful transformation efforts, the leadership coalition grows and grows over time. But whenever some minimum mass is not achieved early in the effort, nothing much worthwhile happens.

It is often said that major change is impossible unless the head of the organization is an active supporter. What I am talking about goes far beyond that. In successful transformations, the chairman or president or division general manager, plus another 5 or 15 or 50 people, come together and develop a shared commitment to excellent performance through renewal. In my experience, this group never includes all of the company's most senior executives because some people just won't buy in, at least not at first. But in the most successful cases, the coalition is always pretty powerful—in terms of titles, information and expertise, reputations and relationships.

In both small and large organizations, a successful guiding team may consist of only three to five people during the first year of a renewal effort. But in big companies, the coalition needs to grow to the 20 to 50 range before much progress can be made in phase three and beyond. Senior managers always form the core of the group. But sometimes you find board members, a representative from a key customer, or even a powerful union leader.

Eight Steps to Transforming Your Organization

Establishing a Sense of Urgency   **1**
Examining market and competitive realities
Identifying and discussing crises, potential crises, or major opportunities

⬇

Forming a Powerful Guiding Coalition   **2**
Assembling a group with enough power to lead the change effort
Encouraging the group to work together as a team

⬇

Creating a Vision   **3**
Creating a vision to help direct the change effort
Developing strategies for achieving that vision

⬇

Communicating the Vision   **4**
Using every vehicle possible to communicate the new vision and
strategies
Teaching new behaviors by the example of the guiding coalition

⬇

Empowering Others to Act on the Vision   **5**
Getting rid of obstacles to change
Changing systems or structures that seriously undermine the vision
Encouraging risk taking and nontraditional ideas, activities, and
actions

⬇

Planning for and Creating Short-Term Wins   **6**
Planning for visible performance improvements
Creating those improvements
Recognizing and rewarding employees involved in the improvements

⬇

Consolidating Improvements and Producing Still More Change   **7**
Using increased credibility to change systems, structures, and
policies that don't fit the vision
Hiring, promoting, and developing employees who can implement
the vision
Reinvigorating the process with new projects, themes, and change
agents

⬇

Institutionalizing New Approaches   **8**
Articulating the connections between the new behaviors and corporate
success
Developing the means to ensure leadership development and
succession

Because the guiding coalition includes members who are not part of senior management, it tends to operate outside of the normal hierarchy by definition. This can be awkward, but it is clearly necessary. If the existing hierarchy were working well, there would be no need for a major transformation. But since the current system is not working, reform generally demands activity outside of formal boundaries, expectations, and protocol.

A high sense of urgency within the managerial ranks helps enormously in putting a guiding coalition together. But more is usually required. Someone needs to get these people together, help them develop a shared assessment of their company's problems and opportunities, and create a minimum level of trust and communication. Off-site retreats, for two or three days, are one popular vehicle for accomplishing this task. I have seen many groups of 5 to 35 executives attend a series of these retreats over a period of months.

Companies that fail in phase two usually underestimate the difficulties of producing change and thus the importance of a powerful guiding coalition. Sometimes they have no history of teamwork at the top and therefore undervalue the importance of this type of coalition. Sometimes they expect the team to be led

In failed transformations, you often find plenty of plans and programs, but no vision.

by a staff executive from human resources, quality, or strategic planning instead of a key line manager. No matter how capable or dedicated the staff head, groups without strong line leadership never achieve the power that is required.

Efforts that don't have a powerful enough guiding coalition can make apparent progress for a while. But, sooner or later, the opposition gathers itself together and stops the change.

Error #3: Lacking a Vision

In every successful transformation effort that I have seen, the guiding coalition develops a picture of the future that is relatively easy to communicate and appeals to customers, stockholders, and employees. A vision always goes beyond the numbers that are typically found in five-year plans. A vision says something that helps clarify the direction in which an organization needs to move. Sometimes the first draft comes mostly from a single individual. It is usually a bit blurry, at least initially. But after the coalition works at it for 3 or 5 or even 12 months, something much better emerges through their tough analytical thinking and a little dreaming. Eventually, a strategy for achieving that vision is also developed.

In one midsize European company, the first pass at a vision contained two-thirds of the basic ideas that were in the final product. The concept of global reach was in the initial version from the beginning. So was the idea of becoming preeminent in certain businesses. But one central idea in the final version—getting out of low value-added activities—came only after a series of discussions over a period of several months.

Without a sensible vision, a transformation effort can easily dissolve into a list of confusing and incompatible projects that can take the organization in the wrong direction or nowhere at all. Without a sound vision, the reengineering project in the accounting department, the new 360-degree performance appraisal from the human resources department, the plant's quality program, the cultural change project in the sales force will not add up in a meaningful way.

In failed transformations, you often find plenty of plans and directives and programs, but no vision. In one case, a company gave out four-inch-thick notebooks describing its change effort. In mind-numbing detail, the books spelled out procedures, goals, methods, and deadlines. But nowhere was there a clear and compelling statement of where all this was leading. Not surprisingly, most of the employees with whom I talked were either confused or alienated. The big, thick books did not rally them together or inspire change. In fact, they probably had just the opposite effect.

In a few of the less successful cases that I have seen, management had a sense of direction, but it was too complicated or blurry to be useful. Recently, I asked an executive in a midsize company to describe his vision and received in return a barely comprehensible 30-minute lecture. Buried in his answer were the basic elements of a sound vision. But they were buried—deeply.

A vision says something that clarifies the direction in which an organization needs to move.

A useful rule of thumb: if you can't communicate the vision to someone in five minutes or less and get a reaction that signifies both understanding and interest, you are not yet done with this phase of the transformation process.

Error #4: Undercommunicating the Vision by a Factor of Ten

I've seen three patterns with respect to communication, all very common. In the first, a group actually does de-

velop a pretty good transformation vision and then pro-
ceeds to communicate it by holding a single meeting or
sending out a single communication. Having used about
.0001% of the yearly intracompany communication, the
group is startled that few people seem to understand the
new approach. In the second pattern, the head of the organization spends a considerable amount of time making
speeches to employee groups, but most people still don't
get it (not surprising, since vision captures only .0005% of
the total yearly communication). In the third pattern,
much more effort goes into newsletters and speeches, but
some very visible senior executives still behave in ways
that are antithetical to the vision. The net result is that
cynicism among the troops goes up, while belief in the
communication goes down.

Transformation is impossible unless hundreds or
thousands of people are willing to help, often to the
point of making short-term sacrifices. Employees will
not make sacrifices, even if they are unhappy with the
status quo, unless they believe that useful change is possible. Without credible communication, and a lot of it,
the hearts and minds of the troops are never captured.

This fourth phase is particularly challenging if the
short-term sacrifices include job losses. Gaining understanding and support is tough when downsizing is a part
of the vision. For this reason, successful visions usually
include new growth possibilities and the commitment to
treat fairly anyone who is laid off.

Executives who communicate well incorporate messages into their hour-by-hour activities. In a routine
discussion about a business problem, they talk about
how proposed solutions fit (or don't fit) into the bigger
picture. In a regular performance appraisal, they talk
about how the employee's behavior helps or undermines the vision. In a review of a division's quarterly

performance, they talk not only about the numbers but also about how the division's executives are contributing to the transformation. In a routine Q&A with employees at a company facility, they tie their answers back to renewal goals.

In more successful transformation efforts, executives use all existing communication channels to broadcast the vision. They turn boring and unread company newsletters into lively articles about the vision. They take ritualistic and tedious quarterly management meetings and turn them into exciting discussions of the transformation. They throw out much of the company's generic management education and replace it with courses that focus on business problems and the new vision. The guiding principle is simple: use every possible channel, especially those that are being wasted on nonessential information.

Perhaps even more important, most of the executives I have known in successful cases of major change learn to "walk the talk." They consciously attempt to become a living symbol of the new corporate culture. This is often not easy. A 60-year-old plant manager who has spent precious little time over 40 years thinking about customers will not suddenly behave in a customer-oriented way. But I have witnessed just such a person change, and change a great deal. In that case, a high level of urgency helped. The fact that the man was a part

Too often, an employee understands the new vision and wants to make it happen. But something appears to be blocking the path.

of the guiding coalition and the vision-creation team also helped. So did all the communication, which kept reminding him of the desired behavior, and all the feedback from his peers and subordinates, which helped him see when he was not engaging in that behavior.

Communication comes in both words and deeds, and the latter are often the most powerful form. Nothing undermines change more than behavior by important individuals that is inconsistent with their words.

Error #5: Not Removing Obstacles to the New Vision

Successful transformations begin to involve large numbers of people as the process progresses. Employees are emboldened to try new approaches, to develop new ideas, and to provide leadership. The only constraint is that the actions fit within the broad parameters of the overall vision. The more people involved, the better the outcome.

To some degree, a guiding coalition empowers others to take action simply by successfully communicating the new direction. But communication is never sufficient by itself. Renewal also requires the removal of obstacles. Too often, an employee understands the new vision and wants to help make it happen. But an elephant appears to be blocking the path. In some cases, the elephant is in the person's head, and the challenge is to convince the individual that no external obstacle exists. But in most cases, the blockers are very real.

Sometimes the obstacle is the organizational structure: narrow job categories can seriously undermine efforts to increase productivity or make it very difficult even to think about customers. Sometimes compensation or performance-appraisal systems make people choose between the new vision and their own self-interest. Perhaps worst of all are bosses who refuse to change and who make demands that are inconsistent with the overall effort.

One company began its transformation process with much publicity and actually made good progress through the fourth phase. Then the change effort ground to a halt because the officer in charge of the company's largest division was allowed to undermine most of the new initiatives. He paid lip service to the process but did not change his behavior or encourage his managers to change. He did not reward the unconventional ideas called for in the vision. He allowed human resource systems to remain intact even when they were clearly inconsistent with the new ideals. I think the officer's motives were complex. To some degree, he did not believe the company needed major change. To some degree, he felt personally threatened by all the change. To some degree, he was afraid that he could not produce both change and the expected operating profit. But despite the fact that they backed the renewal effort, the other officers did virtually nothing to stop the one blocker. Again, the reasons were complex. The company had no history of confronting problems like this. Some people were afraid of the officer. The CEO was concerned that he might lose a talented executive. The net result was disastrous. Lower level managers concluded that senior management had lied to them about their commitment to renewal, cynicism grew, and the whole effort collapsed.

Worst of all are bosses who refuse to change and who make demands that are inconsistent with the overall effort.

In the first half of a transformation, no organization has the momentum, power, or time to get rid of all obstacles. But the big ones must be confronted and removed. If the blocker is a person, it is important that he or she be treated fairly and in a way that is consistent with the new vision. But action is essential, both to empower others and to maintain the credibility of the change effort as a whole.

Error #6: Not Systematically Planning for and Creating Short-Term Wins

Real transformation takes time, and a renewal effort risks losing momentum if there are no short-term goals to meet and celebrate. Most people won't go on the long march unless they see compelling evidence within 12 to 24 months that the journey is producing expected results. Without short-term wins, too many people give up or actively join the ranks of those people who have been resisting change.

One to two years into a successful transformation effort, you find quality beginning to go up on certain indices or the decline in net income stopping. You find some successful new product introductions or an upward shift in market share. You find an impressive productivity improvement or a statistically higher customer-satisfaction rating. But whatever the case, the win is unambiguous. The result is not just a judgment call that can be discounted by those opposing change.

Creating short-term wins is different from hoping for short-term wins. The latter is passive, the former active. In a successful transformation, managers actively look for ways to obtain clear performance improvements, establish goals in the yearly planning system, achieve the objectives, and reward the people involved with recognition, promotions, and even money. For example, the guiding coalition at a U.S. manufacturing company produced a highly visible and successful new product introduction about 20 months after the start of its renewal effort. The new product was selected about six months into the effort because it met multiple criteria: it could be designed and launched in a relatively short period; it could be handled by a small team of people who were devoted to the new vision; it had upside potential; and the new product-development team could operate outside the established departmental structure without practical problems. Little was left to chance, and the win boosted the credibility of the renewal process.

Managers often complain about being forced to produce short-term wins, but I've found that pressure can be a useful element in a change effort. When it becomes clear to people that major change will take a long time, urgency levels can drop. Commitments to produce short-term wins help keep the urgency level up and force detailed analytical thinking that can clarify or revise visions.

Error #7: Declaring Victory Too Soon

After a few years of hard work, managers may be tempted to declare victory with the first clear performance improvement. While celebrating a win is fine, declaring the war won can be catastrophic. Until changes sink deeply into a company's culture, a process that can take five to ten years, new approaches are fragile and subject to regression.

In the recent past, I have watched a dozen change efforts operate under the reengineering theme. In all but two cases, victory was declared and the expensive consultants were paid and thanked when the first major project was completed after two to three years. Within two more years, the useful changes that had been introduced slowly disappeared. In two of the ten cases, it's hard to find any trace of the reengineering work today.

Over the past 20 years, I've seen the same sort of thing happen to huge quality projects, organizational development efforts, and more. Typically, the problems start early in the process: the urgency level is not intense enough, the guiding coalition is not powerful enough, and the vision is not clear enough. But it is the premature victory celebration that kills momentum. And then the powerful forces associated with tradition take over.

While celebrating a win is fine, declaring the war won can be catastrophic. Core ideology provides the glue that holds an organization together through time.

Ironically, it is often a combination of change initiators and change resistors that creates the premature victory celebration. In their enthusiasm over a clear sign of progress, the initiators go overboard. They are then joined by resistors, who are quick to spot any opportunity to stop change. After the celebration is over, the resistors point to the victory as a sign that the war has been won and the troops should be sent home. Weary troops allow themselves to be convinced that they won. Once home, the foot soldiers are reluctant to climb back on the ships. Soon thereafter, change comes to a halt, and tradition creeps back in.

Instead of declaring victory, leaders of successful efforts use the credibility afforded by short-term wins to tackle even bigger problems. They go after systems and structures that are not consistent with the transformation vision and have not been confronted before. They pay great attention to who is promoted, who is hired, and how people are developed. They include new reengineering projects that are even bigger in scope than the initial ones. They understand that renewal efforts take not months but years. In fact, in one of the most successful transformations that I have ever seen, we quantified the amount of change that occurred each year over a seven-year period. On a scale of one (low) to ten (high), year one received a two, year two a four, year three a three, year four a seven, year five an eight, year six a four, and year seven a two. The peak came in year five, fully 36 months after the first set of visible wins.

Error #8: Not Anchoring Changes in the Corporation's Culture

In the final analysis, change sticks when it becomes "the way we do things around here," when it seeps into the bloodstream of the corporate body. Until new behaviors are rooted in social norms and shared values, they are subject to degradation as soon as the pressure for change is removed.

Two factors are particularly important in institutionalizing change in corporate culture. The first is a conscious attempt to show people how the new approaches, behaviors, and attitudes have helped improve performance. When people are left on their own to make the connections, they sometimes create very inaccurate links. For example, because results improved while charismatic Harry was boss, the troops link his mostly idiosyncratic style with those results instead of seeing how their own improved customer service and productivity were instrumental. Helping people see the right connections requires communication. Indeed, one company was relentless, and it paid off enormously. Time was spent at every major management meeting to discuss why performance was increasing. The company newspaper ran article after article showing how changes had boosted earnings.

The second factor is taking sufficient time to make sure that the next generation of top management really does personify the new approach. If the requirements for promotion don't change, renewal rarely lasts. One bad succession decision at the top of an organization can undermine a decade of hard work. Poor succession decisions are possible when boards of directors are not an integral part of the renewal effort. In at least three instances I have seen, the champion for change was the retiring executive, and although his successor was not a resistor, he was not a change champion. Because the boards did not understand the transformations in any detail, they could not see that their choices were not good fits. The retiring executive in one case tried unsuccessfully to talk his board into a less seasoned candidate who better personified the transformation. In the other two cases, the CEOs did not resist the boards' choices, because they felt the transformation could not be undone by their successors. They were wrong. Within two years, signs of renewal began to disappear at both companies.

T HERE ARE STILL MORE mistakes that people make, but these eight are the big ones. I realize that in a short article everything is made to sound a bit too simplistic. In reality, even successful change efforts are messy and full of surprises. But just as a relatively simple vision is needed to guide people through a major change, so a vision of the change process can reduce the error rate. And fewer errors can spell the difference between success and failure.

Originally published in March–April 1995
Reprint 95204

Building Your Company's Vision

JAMES C. COLLINS AND JERRY I. PORRAS

Executive Summary

COMPANIES THAT ENJOY ENDURING SUCCESS have a core purpose and core values that remain fixed while their strategies and practices endlessly adapt to a changing world. The rare ability to balance continuity and change—requiring a consciously practiced discipline—is closely linked to the ability to develop a vision. Vision provides guidance about what to preserve and what to change. A new prescriptive framework adds clarity and rigor to the vague and fuzzy vision concepts at large today.

The framework has two principal parts: core *ideology* and *envisioned future*. Core ideology combines an organization's core values and core purpose. It's the glue that holds a company together as it grows and changes. Core values are an organization's essential and enduring tenets—the values it would hold even if

they became a competitive disadvantage; <u>core purpose</u>
<u>is the organization's fundamental reason for being.</u>

The second component of the vision framework is the
envisioned future. First, a company must identify bold
stretch goals; then it should articulate vivid descriptions
of what it will mean to achieve them. Henry Ford set the
goal of democratizing the automobile, then told the
world, "When I'm through . . . everyone will have one.
The horse will have disappeared from our highways"—
an imaginative stretch for the time.

Unfortunately, the usual vision statement is fuzzy and
inspires only boredom. But managers who master a discovery process to identify core ideology can link their
vision statements to the fundamental dynamic that motivates truly visionary companies—that is, the dynamic of
preserving the core and stimulating progress.

COMPANIES THAT ENJOY ENDURING SUCCESS
have core values and a core purpose that remain fixed
while their business strategies and practices endlessly
adapt to a changing world. The dynamic of preserving
the core while stimulating progress is the reason that
companies such as Hewlett-Packard, 3M, Johnson &
Johnson, Procter & Gamble, Merck, Sony, Motorola,
and Nordstrom became elite institutions able to renew
themselves and achieve superior long-term performance. Hewlett-Packard employees have long known
that radical change in operating practices, cultural
norms, and business strategies does not mean losing
the spirit of the HP Way—the company's core principles. Johnson & Johnson continually questions its
structure and revamps its processes while preserving

the ideals embodied in its credo. In 1996, 3M sold off several of its large mature businesses—a dramatic move that surprised the business press—to refocus on its enduring core purpose of solving unsolved problems innovatively. We studied companies such as these in our research for *Built to Last: Successful Habits of Visionary Companies* and found that they have outperformed the general stock market by a factor of 12 since 1925.

Truly great companies understand the difference between what should never change and what should be open for change, between what is genuinely sacred and what is not. This rare ability to manage continuity and change—requiring a consciously practiced discipline—is closely linked to the ability to develop a vision. Vision provides guidance about what core to preserve and what future to stimulate progress toward. But *vision* has become one of the most overused and least understood words in the language, conjuring up different images for different people: of deeply held values, outstanding achievement, societal bonds, exhilarating goals, motivating forces, or raisons d'être. We recommend a conceptual framework to define vision, add clarity and rigor to the vague and fuzzy concepts swirling around that trendy term, and give practical guidance for articulating a coherent vision within an organization. It is a prescriptive framework rooted in six years of research and refined and tested by our ongoing work with executives from a great variety of organizations around the world.

A well-conceived vision consists of two major components: *core ideology* and *envisioned future*. (See the exhibit "Articulating a Vision.") Core ideology, the yin in our scheme, defines what we stand for and why we exist.

Yin is unchanging and complements yang, the envisioned future. The envisioned future is what we aspire to become, to achieve, to create—something that will require significant change and progress to attain.

Core Ideology

Core ideology defines the enduring character of an organization—a consistent identity that transcends product or market life cycles, technological breakthroughs, management fads, and individual leaders. In fact, the most lasting and significant contribution of those who build visionary companies is the core ideology. As Bill Hewlett said about his longtime friend and business partner David Packard upon Packard's death not long ago, "As far as the company is concerned, the greatest thing he

Articulating a Vision

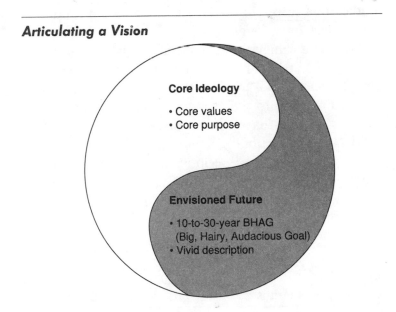

left behind him was a code of ethics known as the HP Way." HP's core ideology, which has guided the company since its inception more than 50 years ago, includes a deep respect for the individual, a dedication to affordable quality and reliability, a commitment to community responsibility (Packard himself bequeathed his $4.3 billion of Hewlett-Packard stock to a charitable foundation), and a view that the company exists to make technical contributions for the advancement and welfare of humanity. Company builders such as David Packard, Masaru Ibuka of Sony, George Merck of Merck, William McKnight of 3M, and Paul Galvin of Motorola understood that it is more important to know who you are than where you are going, for where you are going will change as the world around you changes. Leaders die, products become obsolete, markets change, new technologies emerge, and management fads come and go, but core ideology in a great company endures as a source of guidance and inspiration.

Core ideology provides the glue that holds an organization together through time.

Core ideology provides the glue that holds an organization together as it grows, decentralizes, diversifies, expands globally, and develops workplace diversity. Think of it as analogous to the principles of Judaism that held the Jewish people together for centuries without a homeland, even as they spread throughout the Diaspora. Or think of the truths held to be self-evident in the Declaration of Independence, or the enduring ideals and principles of the scientific community that bond scientists from every nationality together in the common purpose of advancing human knowledge. Any effective vision must embody the core ideology of the organization, which in turn consists of two distinct parts: core values, a system of guiding principles and tenets; and core purpose, the organization's most fundamental reason for existence.

CORE VALUES

Core values are the essential and enduring tenets of an organization. A small set of timeless guiding principles, core values require no external justification; they have *intrinsic* value and importance to those inside the organization. The Walt Disney Company's core values of imagination and wholesomeness stem not from market requirements but from the founder's inner belief that imagination and wholesomeness should be nurtured for their own sake. William Procter and James Gamble didn't instill in P&G's culture a focus on product excellence merely as a strategy for success but as an almost religious tenet. And that value has been passed down for more than 15 decades by P&G people. Service to the customer—even to the point of subservience—is a way of life at Nordstrom that traces its roots back to 1901, eight decades before customer service programs became stylish. For Bill Hewlett and David Packard, respect for the individual was first and foremost a deep personal value; they didn't get it from a book or hear it from a management guru. And Ralph S. Larsen, CEO of Johnson & Johnson, puts it this way: "The core values embodied in our credo might be a competitive advantage, but that is not *why* we have them. We have them because they define for us what we stand for, and we would hold them even if they became a competitive disadvantage in certain situations."

The point is that a great company decides for itself what values it holds to be core, largely independent of the current environment, competitive requirements, or management fads. Clearly, then, there is no universally right set of core values. A company need not have as its core value customer service (Sony doesn't) or respect for the individual (Disney doesn't) or quality (Wal-Mart Stores doesn't) or market focus (HP doesn't) or teamwork (Nordstrom doesn't). A company might have operating practices and business strategies around those qualities without having them at the essence of its being. Furthermore, great companies need not have likable or humanistic core values, although many do. The key is not *what* core values an organization has but that it has core values at all.

Companies tend to have only a few core values, usually between three and five. In fact, we found that none of the visionary companies we studied in our book had more than five: most had only three or four. (See "Core Values Are a Company's Essential Tenets" on page 50.) And, indeed, we should expect that. Only a few values can be truly *core*—that is, so fundamental and deeply held that they will change seldom, if ever.

To identify the core values of your own organization, push with relentless honesty to define what values are truly central. If you articulate more than five or six, chances are that you are confusing core values (which do not change) with operating practices, business strategies, or cultural norms (which should be open to change). Remember, the values must stand the test of time. After you've drafted a preliminary list of the core values, ask about each one, If the circumstances changed and *penalized* us for holding this core value, would we still keep it? If you can't honestly answer yes, then the value is not core and should be dropped from consideration.

A high-technology company wondered whether it should put quality on its list of core values. The CEO asked, "Suppose in ten years quality doesn't make a hoot of difference in our markets. Suppose the only thing that matters is sheer speed and horsepower but not quality. Would we still want to put quality on our list of core values?" The members of the management team looked around at one another and finally said no. Quality stayed in the strategy of the company, and quality-improvement programs remained in place as a mechanism for stimulating progress; but quality did not make the list of core values.

The same group of executives then wrestled with leading-edge innovation as a core value. The CEO asked, "Would we keep innovation on the list as a core value, no matter how the world around us changed?" This time, the management team gave a resounding yes. The managers' outlook might be summarized as, "We always want to do leading-edge innovation. That's who we are. It's really important to us and always will be. No matter what. And if our current markets don't value it, we will find markets that do." Leading-edge innovation went on the list and will stay there. A company should not change its core values in response to market changes; rather, it should change markets, if necessary, to remain true to its core values.

Who should be involved in articulating the core values varies with the size, age, and geographic dispersion of the company, but in many situations we have recommended what we call a *Mars Group*. It works like this: Imagine that you've been asked to re-create the very best attributes of your organization on another planet but you have seats on the rocket ship for only five to seven people. Whom should you send? Most likely, you'll choose the people who have a gut-level understanding of your core values, the highest level of credibility with their peers, and the highest levels of competence. We'll often ask people brought together to work on core values to nominate a Mars Group of five to seven individuals (not necessarily all from the assembled group). Invariably, they end up selecting highly credible representatives who do a super job of articulating the core values precisely because they are exemplars of those values—a representative slice of the company's genetic code.

Even global organizations composed of people from widely diverse cultures can identify a set of shared core values. The secret is to work from the individual to the organization. People involved in articulating the core values need to answer several questions: What core values do you personally bring to your work? (These should be so fundamental that you would hold them regardless of whether or not they were rewarded.) What would you tell your children are the core values that you hold at work and that you hope they will hold when they become working adults? If you awoke tomorrow morning with enough money to retire for the rest of your life, would you continue to live those core values? Can you envision them being as valid for you 100 years from now as they are today? Would you want to hold those core values, even if at some point one or more of them became a competitive disadvantage? If you were to start a new organization tomorrow in a different line of work, what core values would you build into the new organization regardless of its industry? The last three questions are particularly important because they make the crucial distinction between enduring core values that should not change and practices and strategies that should be changing all the time.

CORE PURPOSE

Core purpose, the second part of core ideology, is the organization's reason for being. An effective purpose reflects people's idealistic motivations for doing the company's work. It doesn't just describe the organization's output or target customers; it captures the soul of the organization. (See "Core Purpose Is a Company's Reason for Being" on page 51.) Purpose, as illustrated by a speech David Packard gave to HP employees in 1960, gets at the deeper reasons for an organization's existence beyond just making money. Packard said,

> I want to discuss why a company exists in the first place. In other words, why are we here? I think many people assume, wrongly, that a company exists simply to make money. While this is an important result of a company's existence, we have to go deeper and find the real reasons for our being. As we investigate this, we inevitably come to the conclusion that a group of people get together and exist as an institution that we call a company so they are able to accomplish something collectively that they could not accomplish separately—they make a contribution to society, a phrase which sounds trite but is fundamental. . . . You can look around [in the general business world and] see people who are interested in money and nothing else, but the underlying drives come largely from a desire to do something else: to make a product, to give a service—generally to do something which is of value.[1]

Purpose (which should last at least 100 years) should not be confused with specific goals or business strategies (which should change many times in 100 years). Whereas you might achieve a goal or complete a strategy, you cannot fulfill a purpose; it is like a guiding star on the horizon—forever pursued but never reached. Yet although purpose itself does not change, it does inspire change. The very fact that purpose can never be fully realized means that an organization can never stop stimulating change and progress.

In identifying purpose, some companies make the mistake of simply describing their current product lines or customer segments. We do not consider the following statement to reflect an effective purpose: "We exist to fulfill our government charter and participate in the secondary mortgage market by packaging mortgages into investment securities." The statement is merely descriptive. A far more effective statement of purpose would be that expressed by the executives of the Federal National Mortgage Association, Fannie Mae: "To strengthen the social fabric by continually democratizing home ownership." The secondary mortgage market as we know it might not even exist in 100 years, but strengthening the

> *Core ideology consists of core values and core purpose. Core purpose is a raison d'être, not a goal or business strategy.*

social fabric by continually democratizing home ownership can be an enduring purpose, no matter how much the world changes. Guided and inspired by this purpose, Fannie Mae launched in the early 1990s a series of bold initiatives, including a program to develop new systems for reducing mortgage underwriting costs by 40% in five years; programs to eliminate discrimination in the lending process (backed by $5 billion in underwriting experiments); and an audacious goal to provide, by the year

2000, $1 trillion targeted at 10 million families that had traditionally been shut out of home ownership—minorities, immigrants, and low-income groups.

Similarly, 3M defines its purpose not in terms of adhesives and abrasives but as the perpetual quest to solve unsolved problems innovatively—a purpose that is always leading 3M into new fields. McKinsey & Company's purpose is not to do management consulting but to help corporations and governments be more successful: in 100 years, it might involve methods other than consulting. Hewlett-Packard doesn't exist to make electronic test and measurement equipment but to make technical contributions that improve people's lives—a purpose that has led the company far afield from its origins in electronic instruments. Imagine if Walt Disney had conceived of his company's purpose as to make cartoons, rather than to make people happy; we probably wouldn't have Mickey Mouse, Disneyland, EPCOT Center, or the Anaheim Mighty Ducks Hockey Team.

One powerful method for getting at purpose is the *five whys*. Start with the descriptive statement We make X products or We deliver X services, and then ask, Why is that important? five times. After a few whys, you'll find that you're getting down to the fundamental purpose of the organization.

We used this method to deepen and enrich a discussion about purpose when we worked with a certain market-research company. The executive team first met for several hours and generated the following statement of purpose for their organization: To provide the best market-research data available. We then asked the following question: Why is it important to provide the best market-research data available? After some discussion, the executives answered in a way that reflected a deeper sense of their organization's purpose: To provide the best market-research data available so that our customers will understand their markets better than they could otherwise. A further discussion let team members realize that their sense of self-worth came not just from helping customers understand their markets better but also from making a *contribution* to their customers' success. This introspection eventually led the company to identify its purpose as: To contribute to our customers' success by helping them understand their markets. With this purpose in mind, the company now frames its product decisions not with the question Will it sell? but with the question Will it make a contribution to our customers' success?

The five whys can help companies in any industry frame their work in a more meaningful way. An asphalt and gravel company might begin by saying, We make gravel and asphalt products. After a few whys, it could conclude that making asphalt and gravel is important because the quality of the infrastructure plays a vital role in people's safety and experience; because driving on a pitted road is annoying and dangerous; because 747s cannot land safely on runways built with poor workmanship or inferior concrete; because buildings with substandard materials weaken with time and crumble in earthquakes. From such introspection may emerge this purpose: To make people's lives better by improving the quality of man-made structures. With a sense of purpose very much along those lines, Granite Rock Company of Watsonville, California, won the Malcolm Baldrige

Listen to people in truly great companies talk about their achievements—you will hear little about earnings per share.

National Quality Award—not an easy feat for a small rock quarry and asphalt company. And Granite Rock has gone on to be one of the most progressive and exciting companies we've encountered in *any* industry.

Notice that none of the core purposes fall into the category "maximize shareholder wealth." A primary role of core purpose is to guide and inspire. Maximizing shareholder wealth does not inspire people at all levels of an organization, and it provides precious little guidance. Maximizing shareholder wealth is the standard off-the-shelf purpose for those organizations that have not yet identified their true core purpose. It is a substitute—and a weak one at that.

When people in great organizations talk about their achievements, they say very little about earnings per share. Motorola people talk about impressive quality improvements and the effect of the products they create on the world. Hewlett-Packard people talk about their technical contributions to the marketplace. Nordstrom people talk about heroic customer service and remarkable individual performance by star salespeople. When a Boeing engineer talks about launching an exciting and revolutionary new aircraft, she does not say, "I put my heart and soul into this project because it would add 37 cents to our earnings per share."

One way to get at the purpose that lies beyond merely maximizing shareholder wealth is to play the "Random Corporate Serial Killer" game. It works like this: Suppose you could sell the company to someone who would pay a price that everyone inside and outside the company agrees is more than fair (even with a very generous set of assumptions about the expected future cash flows of the company). Suppose further that this buyer would guarantee stable employment for all employees at the same pay scale after the purchase but with no guarantee that those jobs would be in the same industry. Finally, suppose the buyer plans to kill the company after the purchase—its products or services would be discontinued, its operations would be shut down, its brand names would be shelved forever, and so on. The company would utterly and completely cease to exist. Would you accept the offer? Why or why not? What would be lost if the company ceased to exist? Why is it important that the company continue to exist? We've found this exercise to be very powerful for helping hard-nosed, financially focused executives reflect on their organization's deeper reasons for being.

Another approach is to ask each member of the Mars Group, How could we frame the purpose of this organization so that if you woke up tomorrow morning with enough money in the bank to retire, you would nevertheless keep working here? What deeper sense of purpose would motivate you to continue to dedicate your precious creative energies to this company's efforts?

As they move into the twenty-first century, companies will need to draw on the full creative energy and talent of their people. But why should people give full measure? As Peter Drucker has pointed out, the best and most dedicated people are ultimately volunteers, for they have the opportunity to do something else with their lives. Confronted with an increasingly mobile society, cynicism about corporate life, and an expanding entrepreneurial segment of the economy, companies more than ever need to have a clear understanding of their purpose in order to make work meaningful and thereby attract, motivate, and retain outstanding people.

Discovering Core Ideology

You do not create or set core ideology. You discover core ideology. You do not deduce it by looking at the external environment. You understand it by looking inside. Ideology has to be authentic. You cannot fake it. Discovering core ideology is not an intellectual exercise. Do not ask, What core values should we hold? Ask instead, What core values do we truly and passionately hold? You should not confuse values that you think the organiza-

You discover core ideology by looking inside. It has to be authentic. You can't fake it.

tion ought to have—but does not—with authentic core values. To do so would create cynicism throughout the organization. ("Who're they try-

ing to kid? We all know that isn't a core value around here!") Aspirations are more appropriate as part of your envisioned future or as part of your strategy, not as part of the core ideology. However, authentic core values that have weakened over time can be considered a legitimate part of the core ideology—as long as you acknowledge to the organization that you must work hard to revive them.

Also be clear that the role of core ideology is to guide and inspire, not to differentiate. Two companies can have the same core values or purpose. Many companies could have the purpose to make technical contributions, but few live it as passionately as Hewlett-Packard. Many companies could have the purpose to preserve and improve human life, but few hold it as deeply as Merck. Many companies could have the core value of heroic customer service, but few create as intense a culture around that value as Nordstrom. Many companies could have the core value of innovation, but few create the powerful alignment mechanisms that stimulate the innovation we see at 3M. The authenticity, the discipline, and the consistency with which the ideology is lived—not the content of the ideology—differentiate visionary companies from the rest of the pack.

Core ideology needs to be meaningful and inspirational only to people inside the organization; it need not be exciting to outsiders. Why not? Because it is the people inside the organization who need to commit to the organizational ideology over the long term. Core ideology can also play a role in determining who is inside and who is not. A clear and well-articulated ideology attracts to the company people whose personal values are compatible with the company's core values; conversely, it repels those whose personal values are incompatible. You cannot impose new core values or purpose on people. Nor are core values and purpose things people can buy into. Executives often ask, How do we get people to share our core ideology? You don't. You can't. Instead, find people who are predisposed to share your core values and purpose; attract and retain those people; and let those who do not share your core values go elsewhere. Indeed, the very process of articulating core ideology may cause some people to leave when they realize that they are not personally compatible with the organization's core. Welcome that outcome. It is certainly desirable to retain within the core ideology a diversity of people and viewpoints. People who share the same core values and purpose do not necessarily all think or look the same.

Don't confuse core ideology itself with core-ideology statements. A company can have a very strong core ideology without a formal statement. For example, Nike has not (to our knowledge) formally articulated a statement of its core purpose. Yet, according to our

observations, Nike has a powerful core purpose that
permeates the entire organization: to experience the
emotion of competition, winning, and crushing competitors. Nike has a campus that seems more like a
shrine to the competitive spirit than a corporate office
complex. Giant photos of Nike heroes cover the walls,
bronze plaques of Nike athletes hang along the Nike
Walk of Fame, statues of Nike athletes stand alongside
the running track that rings the campus, and buildings
honor champions such as Olympic marathoner Joan
Benoit, basketball superstar Michael Jordan, and tennis
pro John McEnroe. Nike people who do not feel stimu-
lated by the competitive spirit and the urge to be fero-
cious simply do not last long in the culture. Even the
company's name reflects a sense of competition: Nike
is the Greek goddess of victory. Thus, although Nike
has not formally articulated its purpose, it clearly has a
strong one.

Identifying core values and purpose is therefore not
an exercise in wordsmithery. Indeed, an organization
will generate a variety of statements over time to
describe the core ideology. In Hewlett-Packard's
archives, we found more than half a dozen distinct versions of the HP Way, drafted by David Packard between
1956 and 1972. All versions stated the same principles,
but the words used varied depending on the era and the
circumstances. Similarly, Sony's core ideology has been
stated many different ways over the company's history.
At its founding, Masaru Ibuka described two key elements of Sony's ideology: "We shall welcome technical
difficulties and focus on highly sophisticated technical
products that have great usefulness for society regardless of the quantity involved; we shall place our main
emphasis on ability, performance, and personal charac-

ter so that each individual can show the best in ability and skill."[2] Four decades later, this same concept appeared in a statement of core ideology called Sony Pioneer Spirit: "Sony is a pioneer and never intends to follow others. Through progress, Sony wants to serve the whole world. It shall be always a seeker of the unknown. . . . Sony has a principle of respecting and encouraging one's ability . . . and always tries to bring out the best in a person. This is the vital force of Sony."[3] Same core values, different words.

You should therefore focus on getting the content right—on capturing the essence of the core values and purpose. The point is not to create a perfect statement but to gain a deep understanding of your organization's core values and purpose, which can then be expressed in a multitude of ways. In fact, we often suggest that once the core has been identified, managers should generate their own statements of the core values and purpose to share with their groups.

Finally, don't confuse core ideology with the concept of core competence. Core competence is a strategic concept that defines your organization's capabilities—what you are particularly good at—whereas core ideology captures what you stand for and why you exist. Core competencies should be well aligned with a company's core ideology and are often rooted in it; but they are not the same thing. For example, Sony has a core competence of miniaturization—a strength that can be strategically applied to a wide array of products and markets. But it does not have a core *ideology* of miniaturization. Sony might not even have miniaturization as part of its strategy in 100 years, but to remain a great company, it will still have the same core values described in the Sony Pioneer Spirit and the same fundamental reason for being—namely, to advance technology for the benefit of the general public. In a visionary company like Sony, core competencies change over the decades, whereas core ideology does not.

Once you are clear about the core ideology, you should feel free to change absolutely *anything* that is not part of it. From then on, whenever someone says something should not change because "it's part of our culture" or "we've always done it that way" or any such excuse, mention this simple rule: If it's not core, it's up for change. The strong version of the rule is, *If it's not core, change it!* Articulating core ideology is just a starting point, however. You also must determine what type of progress you want to stimulate.

Envisioned Future

The second primary component of the vision framework is *envisioned future*. It consists of two parts: a 10-to-30-year audacious goal plus vivid descriptions of what it will be like to achieve the goal. We recognize that the phrase *envisioned future* is somewhat paradoxical. On the one hand, it conveys concreteness—something visible, vivid, and real. On the other hand, it involves a time yet unrealized—with its dreams, hopes, and aspirations.

VISION-LEVEL BHAG

We found in our research that visionary companies often use bold missions—or what we prefer to call *BHAGs* (pronounced BEE-hags and shorthand for Big, Hairy, Audacious Goals)—as a powerful way to stimulate progress. All companies have goals. But there is a difference between merely having a goal and becoming

committed to a huge, daunting challenge—such as
climbing Mount Everest. A true BHAG is clear and compelling, serves as a unifying focal point of effort, and acts
as a catalyst for team
spirit. It has a clear finish line, so the organization can know when it
has achieved the goal;
people like to shoot for
finish lines. A BHAG engages people—it reaches out and
grabs them. It is tangible, energizing, highly focused.
People get it right away; it takes little or no explanation.
For example, NASA's 1960s moon mission didn't need a
committee of wordsmiths to spend endless hours turning the goal into a verbose, impossible-to-remember
mission statement. The goal itself was so easy to grasp—
so compelling in its own right—that it could be said 100
different ways yet be easily understood by everyone.
Most corporate statements we've seen do little to spur
forward movement because they do not contain the
powerful mechanism of a BHAG.

Companies need an audacious 10-to-30-year goal to progress toward an envisioned future.

   Although organizations may have many BHAGs at
different levels operating at the same time, vision
requires a special type of BHAG—a vision-level BHAG
that applies to the entire organization and requires 10 to
30 years of effort to complete. Setting the BHAG that far
into the future requires thinking beyond the current
capabilities of the organization and the current environment. Indeed, inventing such a goal forces an executive
team to be visionary, rather than just strategic or tactical. A BHAG should not be a sure bet—it will have perhaps only a 50% to 70% probability of success—but the
organization must believe that it can reach the goal anyway. A BHAG should require extraordinary effort and

perhaps a little luck. We have helped companies create a vision-level BHAG by advising them to think in terms of four broad categories: target BHAGs, common-enemy BHAGs, role-model BHAGs, and internal-transformation BHAGs. (See "Big, Hairy, Audacious Goals Aid Long-Term Vision" on page 52.)

VIVID DESCRIPTION

In addition to vision-level BHAGs, an envisioned future needs what we call *vivid description*—that is, a vibrant, engaging, and specific description of what it will be like to achieve the BHAG. Think of it as translating the vision from words into pictures, of creating an image that people can carry around in their heads. It is a question of painting a picture with your words. Picture painting is essential for making the 10-to-30-year BHAG tangible in people's minds.

You must translate the vision from words to pictures with a vivid description of what it will be like to achieve your goal.

For example, Henry Ford brought to life the goal of democratizing the automobile with this vivid description: "I will build a motor car for the great multitude. . . . It will be so low in price that no man making a good salary will be unable to own one and enjoy with his family the blessing of hours of pleasure in God's great open spaces. . . . When I'm through, everybody will be able to afford one, and everyone will have one. The horse will have disappeared from our highways, the automobile will be taken for granted . . . [and we will] give a large number of men employment at good wages."

The components-support division of a computer-products company had a general manager who was able to describe vividly the goal of becoming one of the most sought-after divisions in the company: "We will be respected and admired by our peers. . . . Our solutions will be actively sought by the end-product divisions, who will achieve significant product 'hits' in the marketplace largely because of our technical contribution. . . . We will have pride in ourselves. . . . The best up-and-coming people in the company will seek to work in our division. . . . People will give unsolicited feedback that they love what they are doing. . . . [Our own] people will walk on the balls of their feet. . . . [They] will willingly work hard because they want to. . . . Both employees and customers will feel that our division has contributed to their life in a positive way."

In the 1930s, Merck had the BHAG to transform itself from a chemical manufacturer into one of the preeminent drug-making companies in the world, with a research capability to rival any major university. In describing this envisioned future, George Merck said at the opening of Merck's research facility in 1933, "We believe that research work carried on with patience and persistence will bring to industry and commerce new life; and we have faith that in this new laboratory, with the tools we have supplied, science will be advanced, knowledge increased, and human life win ever a greater freedom from suffering and disease. . . . We pledge our every aid that this enterprise shall merit the faith we have in it. Let your light so shine—that those who seek the Truth, that those who toil that this world may be a better place to live in, that those who hold aloft that torch of science and knowledge through these social and economic dark ages, shall take new courage and feel their hands supported."

Passion, emotion, and conviction are essential parts of the vivid description. Some managers are uncomfortable expressing emotion about their dreams, but that's what motivates others. Churchill understood that when he described the BHAG facing Great Britain in 1940. He did not just say, "Beat Hitler." He said, "Hitler knows he will have to break us on this island or lose the war. If we can stand up to him, all Europe may be free, and the life of the world may move forward into broad, sunlit uplands. But if we fail, the whole world, including the United States, including all we have known and cared for, will sink into the abyss of a new Dark Age, made more sinister and perhaps more protracted by the lights of perverted science. Let us therefore brace ourselves to our duties and so bear ourselves that if the British Empire and its Commonwealth last for a thousand years, men will still say, 'This was their finest hour.' "

A FEW KEY POINTS

Don't confuse core ideology and envisioned future. In particular, don't confuse core purpose and BHAGs. Managers often exchange one for the other, mixing the two together or failing to articulate both as distinct items. Core purpose—not some specific goal—is the reason why the organization exists. A BHAG is a clearly articulated goal. Core purpose can never be completed, whereas the BHAG is reachable in 10 to 30 years. Think of the core purpose as the star on the horizon to be chased forever; the BHAG is the mountain to be climbed. Once you have reached its summit, you move on to other mountains.

Identifying core ideology is a discovery process, but setting the envisioned future is a creative process. We find that executives often have a great deal of difficulty coming up with an exciting BHAG. They want to analyze their way into the future. We have found, therefore, that some executives make more progress by starting first with the vivid description and backing from there into the BHAG. This approach involves starting with questions such as, We're sitting here in 20 years; what would we love to see? What should this company look like? What should it feel like to employees? What should it have achieved? If someone writes an article for a major business magazine about this company in 20 years, what will it say? One biotechnology company we worked with had trouble envisioning its future. Said one member of the executive team, "Every time we come up with something for the entire company, it is just too generic to be exciting—something banal like 'advance biotechnology worldwide.' " Asked to paint a picture of the company in 20 years, the executives mentioned such things as "on the cover of *Business Week* as a model success story . . . the *Fortune* most admired top-ten list . . . the best science and business graduates want to work here . . . people on airplanes rave about one of our products to seatmates . . . 20 consecutive years of profitable growth . . . an entrepreneurial culture that has spawned half a dozen new divisions from within . . . management gurus use us as an example of excellent management and progressive thinking," and so on. From this, they were able to set the goal of becoming as well respected as Merck or as Johnson & Johnson in biotechnology.

It makes no sense to analyze whether an envisioned future is the right one. With a creation—and the task is creation of a future, not prediction—there can be no right answer. Did Beethoven create the right Ninth Symphony? Did Shakespeare create the right *Hamlet*? We can't answer these questions; they're nonsense. The envisioned future involves such essential questions as Does it get our juices flowing? Do we find it stimulating? Does it spur forward momentum? Does it get

What's needed is such a big commitment that when people see what the goal will take, there's an almost audible gulp.

people going? The envisioned future should be so exciting in its own right that it would continue to keep the organization motivated even if the leaders who set the goal disappeared. City Bank, the predecessor of Citicorp, had the BHAG "to become the most powerful, the most serviceable, the most far-reaching world financial institution that has ever been"—a goal that generated excitement through multiple generations until it was achieved. Similarly, the NASA moon mission continued to galvanize people even though President John F. Kennedy (the leader associated with setting the goal) died years before its completion.

To create an effective envisioned future requires a certain level of unreasonable confidence and commitment. Keep in mind that a BHAG is not just a goal; it is a Big, Hairy, Audacious Goal. It's not reasonable for a small regional bank to set the goal of becoming "the most powerful, the most serviceable, the most far-reaching world financial institution that has ever been," as City Bank did in 1915. It's not a tepid claim that "we will democratize the automobile," as Henry Ford said. It was almost laughable for Philip Morris—as the sixth-place player with 9% market share in the 1950s—to take on the goal of defeating Goliath RJ Reynolds Tobacco Com-

pany and becoming number one. It was hardly modest
for Sony, as a small, cash-strapped venture, to proclaim
the goal of changing the poor-quality image of Japanese
products around the world. (See "Putting It All Together: Sony in the 1950s" on page 53.) Of course, it's not
only the audacity of the goal but also the level of commitment to the goal that counts. Boeing didn't just envision a future dominated by its commercial jets; it bet the
company on the 707 and, later, on the 747. Nike's people
didn't just talk about the idea of crushing Adidas; they
went on a crusade to fulfill the dream. Indeed, the envisioned future should produce a bit of the "gulp factor":
when it dawns on people what it will take to achieve the
goal, there should be an almost audible gulp.

But what about failure to realize the envisioned
future? In our research, we found that the visionary
companies displayed a remarkable ability to achieve
even their most audacious goals. Ford did democratize
the automobile; Citicorp did become the most far-reaching bank in the world; Philip Morris did rise from sixth
to first and beat RJ Reynolds worldwide; Boeing did
become the dominant commercial aircraft company;
and it looks like Wal-Mart will achieve its $125 billion
goal, even without Sam Walton. In contrast, the comparison companies in our research frequently did not
achieve their BHAGs, if they set them at all. The difference does not lie in setting easier goals: the visionary
companies tended to have even more audacious ambi-
tions. The difference does not lie in charismatic, visionary leadership: the visionary companies often achieved
their BHAGs without such larger-than-life leaders at the
helm. Nor does the difference lie in better strategy: the
visionary companies often realized their goals more by
an organic process of "let's try a lot of stuff and keep

what works" than by well-laid strategic plans. Rather, their success lies in building the strength of their organization as their primary way of creating the future.

Why did Merck become the preeminent drugmaker in the world? Because Merck's architects built the best pharmaceutical research and development organization in the world. Why did Boeing become the dominant commercial aircraft company in the world? Because of its superb engineering and marketing organization, which had the ability to make projects like the 747 a reality. When asked to name the most important decisions that have contributed to the growth and success of Hewlett-Packard, David Packard answered entirely in terms of decisions to build the strength of the organization and its people.

Finally, in thinking about the envisioned future, beware of the We've Arrived Syndrome—a complacent lethargy that arises once an organization has achieved one BHAG and fails to replace it with another. NASA suffered from that syndrome after the successful moon landings. After you've landed on the moon, what do you do for an encore? Ford suffered from the syndrome when, after it succeeded in democratizing the automobile, it failed to set a new goal of equal significance and gave General Motors the opportunity to jump ahead in the 1930s. Apple Computer suffered from the syndrome after achieving the goal of creating a computer that nontechies could use. Start-up companies frequently suffer from the We've Arrived Syndrome after

> *The basic dynamic of visionary companies is to preserve the core and stimulate progress. It is vision that provides the context.*

going public or after reaching a stage in which survival no longer seems in question. An envisioned future helps an organization only as long as it hasn't yet been achieved. In our work with companies, we frequently hear executives say, "It's just not as exciting around here as it used to be; we seem to have lost our momentum." Usually, that kind of remark signals that the organization has climbed one mountain and not yet picked a new one to climb.

Many executives thrash about with mission statements and vision statements. Unfortunately, most of those statements turn out to be a muddled stew of values, goals, purposes, philosophies, beliefs, aspirations, norms, strategies, practices, and descriptions. They are usually a boring, confusing, structurally unsound stream of words that evoke the response "True, but who cares?" Even more problematic, seldom do these statements have a direct link to the fundamental dynamic of visionary companies: preserve the core and stimulate progress. That dynamic, not vision or mission statements, is the primary engine of enduring companies. Vision simply provides the context for bringing this dynamic to life. Building a visionary company requires 1% vision and 99% alignment. When you have superb alignment, a visitor could drop in from outer space and infer your vision from the operations and activities of the company without ever reading it on paper or meeting a single senior executive.

Creating alignment may be your most important work. But the first step will always be to recast your vision or mission into an effective context for building a visionary company. If you do it right, you shouldn't have to do it again for at least a decade.

Core Values Are a Company's Essential Tenets

Merck

- Corporate social responsibility
- Unequivocal excellence in all aspects of the company
- Science-based innovation
- Honesty and integrity
- Profit, but profit from work that benefits humanity

Nordstrom

- Service to the customer above all else
- Hard work and individual productivity
- Never being satisfied
- Excellence in reputation; being part of something special

Philip Morris

- The right to freedom of choice
- Winning—beating others in a good fight
- Encouraging individual initiative
- Opportunity based on merit; no one is entitled to anything
- Hard work and continuous self-improvement

Sony

- Elevation of the Japanese culture and national status
- Being a pioneer—not following others; doing the impossible
- Encouraging individual ability and creativity

Walt Disney

- No cynicism
- Nurturing and promulgation of "wholesome American values"
- Creativity, dreams, and imagination
- Fanatical attention to consistency and detail
- Preservation and control of the Disney magic

Core Purpose Is a Company's Reason for Being

3M: To solve unsolved problems innovatively

Cargill: To improve the standard of living around the world

Fannie Mae: To strengthen the social fabric by continually democratizing home ownership

Hewlett-Packard: To make technical contributions for the advancement and welfare of humanity

Lost Arrow Corporation: To be a role model and a tool for social change

Pacific Theatres: To provide a place for people to flourish and to enhance the community

Mary Kay Cosmetics: To give unlimited opportunity to women

McKinsey & Company: To help leading corporations and governments be more successful

Merck: To preserve and improve human life

Nike: To experience the emotion of competition, winning, and crushing competitors

Sony: To experience the joy of advancing and applying technology for the benefit of the public

Telecare Corporation: To help people with mental impairments realize their full potential

Wal-Mart: To give ordinary folk the chance to buy the same things as rich people

Walt Disney: To make people happy

Big, Hairy, Audacious Goals Aid Long-Term Vision

Target BHAGs can be quantitative or qualitative

- Become a $125 billion company by the year 2000 (Wal-Mart, 1990)
- Democratize the automobile (Ford Motor Company, early 1900s)
- Become the company most known for changing the worldwide poor-quality image of Japanese products (Sony, early 1950s)
- Become the most powerful, the most serviceable, the most far-reaching world financial institution that has ever been (City Bank, predecessor to Citicorp, 1915)
- Become the dominant player in commercial aircraft and bring the world into the jet age (Boeing, 1950)

Common-enemy BHAGs involve David-versus-Goliath thinking

- Knock off RJR as the number one tobacco company in the world (Philip Morris, 1950s)
- Crush Adidas (Nike, 1960s)
- *Yamaha wo tsubusu!* We will destroy Yamaha! (Honda, 1970s)

Role-model BHAGs suit up-and-coming organizations

- Become the Nike of the cycling industry (Giro Sport Design, 1986)
- Become as respected in 20 years as Hewlett-Packard is today (Watkins-Johnson, 1996)
- Become the Harvard of the West (Stanford University, 1940s)

Internal-transformation BHAGs suit large, established organizations

- Become number one or number two in every market we serve and revolutionize this company to have the strengths of a big company combined with the leanness and agility of a small company (General Electric Company, 1980s)
- Transform this company from a defense contractor into the best diversified high-technology company in the world (Rockwell, 1995)
- Transform this division from a poorly respected internal products supplier to one of the most respected, exciting, and sought-after divisions in the company (Components Support Division of a computer products company, 1989)

Putting It All Together: Sony in the 1950s

Core Ideology

Core Values

- Elevation of the Japanese culture and national status
- Being a pioneer—not following others; doing the impossible
- Encouraging individual ability and creativity

Purpose

To experience the sheer joy of innovation and the application of technology for the benefit and pleasure of the general public

Envisioned Future

BHAG

Become the company most known for changing the worldwide poor-quality image of Japanese products

Vivid Description

We will create products that become pervasive around the world. . . . We will be the first Japanese company to go into the U.S. market and distribute directly. . . . We will succeed with innovations that U.S. companies have failed at—such as the transistor radio. . . . Fifty years from now, our brand name will be as well known as any in the world . . . and will signify innovation and quality that rival the most innovative companies anywhere. . . . "Made in Japan" will mean something fine, not something shoddy.

Notes

1. David Packard, speech given to Hewlett-Packard's training group on March 8, 1960; courtesy of Hewlett-Packard Archives.

2. See Nick Lyons, *The Sony Vision* (New York: Crown Publishers, 1976). We also used a translation by our Japanese student Tsuneto Ikeda.

3. Akio Morita, *Made in Japan* (New York: E.P. Dutton, 1986), p. 147.

Originally published in September–October 1996
Reprint 96501

Managing Change

The Art of Balancing

JEANIE DANIEL DUCK

Executive Summary

IT SHOULD COME AS NO SURPRISE that companies are full of "change survivors," people who have learned to live through change programs without actually changing. After all, for change to occur in any organization, each person must think, feel, or do something different. For most executives, this daunting process is unlike any other managerial task they have ever confronted.

Jeanie Duck argues that managers need a new way to think about managing change in today's knowledge organization. Instead of breaking change into small pieces—TQM, process re-engineering, employee empowerment—and then managing these pieces, managers need to think in terms of overseeing a dynamic. Instead of thinking about managing change like operating a machine or treating the human body one ailment at a time, managers must connect and balance all pieces of the change effort.

Managing change is like balancing a mobile. Achieving this critical balance means managing the conversation between the people leading the change effort and those who are expected to implement the new strategies; creating an organizational context in which change can occur; and managing emotional connections, which have traditionally been banned from the workplace but are essential for a successful transformation.

One tool that companies can use is the Transition Management Team, a group of company leaders, reporting to the CEO, who commit all their time and energy to managing change. When the process has stabilized, the TMT disbands. Until then, it oversees the corporate change effort and ensures that leaders and followers work together to create the future.

CHANGE IS INTENSELY PERSONAL. For change to occur in any organization, each individual must think, feel, or do something different. Even in large organizations, which depend on thousands of employees understanding company strategies well enough to translate them into appropriate actions, leaders must win their followers one by one. Think of this as 25,000 people having conversion experiences and ending up at a predetermined place at approximately the same time. Small wonder that corporate change is such a difficult and frustrating item on virtually every company's agenda.

The problem for most executives is that managing change is unlike any other managerial task they have ever confronted. One COO at a large corporation told me that when it comes to handling even the most complex operational problem, he has all the skills he needs. But when it comes to managing change, the model he uses for operational issues doesn't work.

"It's like the company is undergoing five medical procedures at the same time," he told me. "One person's in charge of the root-canal job, someone else is setting the broken foot, another person is working on the displaced shoulder, and still another is getting rid of the gallstone. Each operation is a success, but the patient dies of shock."

The problem is simple: we are using a mechanistic model, first applied to managing physical work, and superimposing it onto the new mental model of today's knowledge organization. We keep breaking change into small pieces and then managing the pieces. This is the legacy of Frederick Winslow Taylor and scientific management. But with change, the task is to manage the dynamic, not the pieces. The challenge is to innovate mental work, not to replicate physical work. The goal is to teach thousands of people how to think strategically, recognize patterns, and anticipate problems and opportunities before they occur.

Managing change isn't like operating a machine or treating the human body one ailment at a time. Both of these activities involve working with a fixed set of relationships. The proper metaphor for managing change is balancing a mobile. Most organizations today find themselves undertaking a number of projects as part of their change effort. An organization may simultaneously be working on TQM, process reengineering, employee empowerment, and several other programs designed to improve performance. But the key to the change effort is not attending to each piece in isolation; it's connecting and balancing all the pieces. In managing change, the critical task is understanding how pieces balance off one another, how changing one element changes the rest, how sequencing and pace affect the whole structure.

One tool that companies can use to provide that critical balance is the Transition Management Team, a group of company leaders, reporting to the CEO, who commit all their time and energy to managing the change process. When that process has stabilized, the TMT disbands; until then, it oversees the corporate change effort. Managing change means managing the conversation between the people leading the change effort and those who are expected to implement the new strategies, managing the organizational context in which change can occur, and managing the emotional connections that are essential for any transformation.

H ERE'S THE WAY most companies approach change: the CEO or division head announces, "We have to make some changes around here. The following people are appointed to a task force to come up with our new design. The task force will report back to me in 90 days."

Task-force members usually agree: keeping everyone in the company informed is a diversion, a luxury they can't afford.

What happens next is predictable. The task force goes to work, closeting itself away in a meeting room, putting in long hours to meet the deadline. The members don't talk with anyone else in the organization. They're involved in trying to work out their own group dynamics and testing a lot of what-ifs. Among themselves, they agree: trying to keep everybody else informed is a diversion, a luxury they can't afford. Once the 90 days are up, and it's time to report to the boss, then the task force will figure out a way to let everyone else know what it accomplished.

This approach virtually guarantees that the change effort will fail. The assumption of the CEO and the task force is, "We haven't said anything yet, so we're not really communicating. We haven't sent any messages."

But the opposite is true. Everything that is or is not done sends a message. The original announcement that change is on its way sends a message. Depending on the company's recent past, the organization may feel only a mild ripple—or an alarm may go off. Even the appointment of the task force by the CEO sends an important message. In any organization, where information is power and access to information is determined by who attends certain meetings, a task force identifies who does and doesn't have power.

When the task force chooses not to inform the rest of the organization about its work, it is saying, "We're busy figuring out your future—we'll tell you what it is when we're ready." Of course, people abhor information vacuums; when there is no ongoing conversation as part of the change process, gossip fills the vacuum. Usually the rumors are much worse and more negative than anything that is actually going on.

When task-force members put off communicating with the rest of the organization, they prevent people from understanding the design principles that guided them, the lessons they learned from previous experience, the trade-offs they had to make. They unwittingly prevent the people who are expected to implement the change from participating or buying in. As a consequence, no matter how good the new design turns out to be, it doesn't produce the expected results.

This scenario is common. I saw it played out at a large company that was considering restructuring its organization and relocating its headquarters. The executive group working on the project never put out a formal announcement. But that didn't mean that other people in the organization didn't know something was going on. The words "Restructuring Committee Meeting" appeared regularly on the calendars the committee members' secretaries kept for them. People noticed that they were spending more time on this project than on any other. And the rumor mill reported that when the committee members came out of their meetings, they looked worried.

The people in the organization had their own interpretation: something big is going on because they're having to spend a lot of time on it. And it must be horrible because they don't want to tell us about it.

At the end of nine months, the executive committee made its formal announcement—and even that was done in a way that minimized the chance for conversation. Each member of the committee went to a different location and read from the same script at a one-hour, companywide meeting held on a Thursday. The announcement was hardly awful: the committee had decided to restructure the company and move its headquarters to another city. There were no layoffs, but those people who wanted a job at headquarters would have to relocate. Out of a company of 35,000, only about 1,500 employees were directly affected by the decision.

After the announcement, there was no time allotted for questions and answers, and there was no discussion about the transition. The executives didn't think it was necessary because they were sending a binder filled with the details to managers in affected areas the following Monday. They figured it would be better to wait until all the information was available than to try to answer questions immediately after the announcement.

When it came time to implement the decision, the company paid the price for its communications mistakes. Managers and workers felt alienated and devalued. Their opinions had never been sought; their concerns and feelings had never been considered. Managers did not feel prepared to handle the barrage of questions they encountered that Monday, and no one was comforted by a binder. Some people voted with their feet and simply did not make the move to the new headquarters. Others were even more destructive: they disengaged from any real effort to make the company successful but stayed on the payroll.

The crucial lesson here is that management is the message. Everything managers say—or don't say—delivers a message. Too many managers assume that communications is a staff function, something for human resources or public relations to take care of. In fact, communications must be a priority for every manager at every level of the company.

This is particularly true during a change effort, when rumors run rampant. It is important for the messages to be consistent, clear, and endlessly repeated. If there is a single rule of communications for leaders, it is this: when you are so sick of talking about something that you can hardly stand it, your message is finally starting to get through.

People in the organization may need to hear a message over and over before they believe that this time, the call for change is not just a whim or a passing fancy. It takes time for people to hear, understand, and believe the message. And if they don't particularly like what they hear, then it takes even more time for them to come to terms with the concept of change.

From the point of view of the leaders, who have been working on the change program for months, the message is already stale. But what counts is the point of view of everyone else in the organization. Have they heard the message? Do they believe it? Do they know what it means? Have they interpreted it for themselves, and have they internalized it?

Until managers have listened, watched, and talked enough to know that the answer to all these questions is yes, they haven't communicated at all.

Accorrding to conventional wisdom, change works like this: You start by getting people to buy into a new corporate vision, thereby changing their attitudes. They will then automatically change their behavior, which will result in improved corporate performance. After seeing this improvement, they will confirm their commitment to the corporate change program, and the success spiral will continue.

By now, the troops have been through so many change programs that they're skeptical.

This may have occurred in some company somewhere. But more typically, managers launching a change program want the troops to get excited; they want their team to have "a winning attitude." So when announcing the program, they "go for love," seeking to get people to believe in the new vision.

Unfortunately, it's not realistic to expect that kind of response in most companies these days. By now, the troops have been through so many of these programs that they're skeptical. Companies today are full of "change survivors," cynical people who've learned how to live through change programs without really changing at all. Their reaction is the opposite of commitment. They say things like, "I'll believe it when I see it," or, "Sure, this sounds great, but what happens when we don't make the numbers?" Of course, there are always some enthusiastic people. All they need is permission to go off and try the new approach. But for the others, the new program is just another management fad in an endless series of management fads.

This reaction from so many employees illustrates the real reason so many change programs fail: this model of change doesn't correspond to reality. In most companies, the real context for change is exactly the opposite. Top management should start by requiring a change of behavior, and when that yields improved performance, the excitement and belief will follow.

The first change in behavior should be that of the top executives. Leaders need to ask themselves, "If we were managing the way we say we want to manage, how would we act? How would we attack our problems? What kind of meetings and conversations would we have? Who would be involved? How would we define, recognize, compensate, and reward appropriate behavior?" As leaders and followers work side by side to develop the answers to these questions, they create their future together.

For example, one popular management technique is to push decision making down to the lowest appropriate level. It sounds simple, deceptively simple. I was present one morning when a newly enlightened CEO went to a factory for an all-employee meeting. He talked about empowerment and candor and the need to put all the issues on the table. He then invited questions from all present about whatever was on their minds. One brave worker raised his hand and asked why it was that the plant manager could be responsible for equipment worth millions of dollars but only have sign-off authority of $5,000.

"Good question!" the CEO instantly responded. "I believe in empowerment so much that I'll make his sign-off authority $1 million."

The worker who had asked the question was impressed. The CEO was elated. The plant manager was terrified. What had he learned that morning that was worth $995,000? Who was going to help him make decisions involving that much money? Could he expect any mercy when he made his first $250,000 mistake? The CEO had made the dramatic gesture of going for love, but he'd neglected the crucial element: he had not prepared the plant manager to handle so much responsibility.

> *Empowerment doesn't mean abandonment. Setting the context for change means understanding what employees do and don't know.*

Empowerment does not mean abandonment. Giving people permission to do something differently is not helpful if they are unable to do it. That permission just sets them up to fail. Setting the context for change means preparing the players, understanding what they do and don't know, working with them, watching their performance, giving them feedback, creating an ongoing dialogue with them.

Compare this CEO's behavior to that of a sales vice president who decided that her regional directors should run their operations independently, as long as business objectives were met and corporate values honored. She discussed this at length with all the directors, who were quite happy with her decision. But on reflection, she realized that some directors were more experienced than others and that she would need to work with each one differently. She then set up one-on-one meetings with each director to find out what his plans were and how he wanted to interact with her. During this round of conversations, she reached explicit agreements with each director about what kinds of decisions or problems he would like help with, how he would update her, and how the directors would keep each other informed. As a result, her role as coach was tailor-made to each person on her team; each plan took into consideration her comfort with each director's abilities as well as each director's desires and preferred management relationship.

Over and over, I've witnessed the same hard truth: When it comes to change, people don't believe in a new direction because they suspend their disbelief. They believe because they're actually seeing behavior, action, and results that lead them to conclude that the program works.

Companies cannot legislate their employees' feelings, but companies do rent their behavior. It sounds crass, but it's true. "Winning attitudes" do make a difference, and it is important to market new ideas and approaches within an organization very carefully. But even that kind of approach to change won't convert the hardened change survivors. With all employees, managers have more leverage over what they do than how they feel.

For DECADES, managers and workers have been told to check their feelings at the door. And that's a big mistake. It's one thing to say that behavior is more accessible to managers than feelings are; it's another thing altogether to say that feelings have no place at work.

Change is fundamentally about feelings; companies that want their workers to contribute with their heads and hearts have to accept that emotions are essential to the new management style. The old management paradigm said that at work people are only permitted to feel emotions that are easily controllable, emotions that can be categorized as "positive." The new management paradigm says that managing people is managing feelings. The issue isn't whether or not people have "negative" emotions; it's how they deal with them. In fact, the most successful change programs reveal that large organizations connect with their people most directly through values—and that values, ultimately, are about beliefs and feelings.

I saw a classic example of this at a large company with over 100,000 employees worldwide, seeking to develop a values statement as a way to bring its people together. The executive team had made an intellectual commitment to the notion of values but had shown little progress over several months—until an accidental breakthrough one day moved them to a different level. The executive team was gathering for a meeting, but the official agenda was delayed. To fill the time, they got into an informal conversation, asking each other the questions, "What helped you form your values? How did you come to realize that you had particular values?"

What started as an informal discussion gradually took over as the agenda for the meeting. As they went around the table, one of the men told a story about his youth in another country and about his grandfather, who had been an important person in his life. The more he talked, the more he remembered what the relationship had meant to him. As he told the story, he started to cry.

In most corporate settings, it is strictly taboo for a senior executive to cry, to show tenderness or grief. This behavior is something that executives avoid at all costs. But at that meeting, when the man started to cry, all the others felt a stronger connection to him. They acknowledged their own feelings toward someone who had played a similar role in their lives. Or they realized that they had missed out by not having had such a relationship.

Out of that discussion came a wider conversation that touched on what they had learned growing up about emotions, human connections, and values and how these qualities shaped their leadership style and behavior within the corporation. Even the men who had looked to affectionate and emotional role models growing up came to realize that in corporate life they steered clear of emotions—because that was the operating norm. Changing that norm became one of the group's explicit targets.

When an organization either denies the validity of emotions in the workplace or seeks to permit only certain kinds of emotions, two things happen. The first is that managers cut themselves off from their own emotional lives. Even more important, they cut off the ideas, solutions, and new perspectives that other people can contribute.

The corollary is when managers are unwilling to let themselves or their employees experience "negative" emotions, no matter how upsetting or difficult the situation may be. It's true that getting a group of people together and allowing them to vent their emotions can initiate a negative spiral. But it's also true that there are simple and effective ways to tell people, "You can visit Pity City, but you aren't allowed to move there."

I saw this process at work in an information systems department of a company that was undergoing a large and complex computer conversion. Rather than denying that the rest of the organization was making huge demands on the department and that everyone was under enormous stress, the project director decided to acknowledge just how difficult the conversion really was. The first thing he did was to have t-shirts made, large enough to fit over people's work clothes. On the front were the words, "Yes, it's hard." On the back it said, "But we can do it."

Once a week, people could visit Pity City. But they weren't allowed to move there.

The project director also scheduled meetings on Tuesday and Friday afternoons with the team and their primary users. For the first 15 minutes, the group would visit Pity City. People would go on and on with the usual gripes that come up at a difficult time. As a group, they could acknowledge just how horrible all this really was— but only for 15 minutes. Then for the next 15 minutes, the meeting became a brag session, where people would showcase all the little victories—the things that had worked, ways they had delighted their customers, problems they had turned into successes. The one rule was that everyone had to participate at least once every week in both the griping and the bragging.

Over the ten months of the project, these sessions built up a remarkable degree of camaraderie among

the team members. One woman, in particular, illustrated why it was important to admit feelings in the
workplace. When the sessions started, this woman told
the project director that she didn't want to participate.
She thought that others may need an emotional
crutch, but she didn't. The supervisor told her that she
still had to participate.

The woman discovered that these meetings did make
a difference in how she felt about her teammates and
her willingness to ask for help. The team came to realize
that the conversion program was hard for everyone.
Moreover, from listening to the complaints, they began
to give each other ideas about ways to handle tough situations. Finally, as they told each other of the little victories, they began to feel like they were part of a winning
team. When the project was over, they felt even better
about themselves and their organization than they had
at the beginning.

O NE OF THE PARADOXES of change is that trust is
hardest to establish when you need it the most. There
are some companies that employees trust. But if a company is in trouble, or if it is in the middle of a change
effort, lack of trust automatically emerges as a serious
barrier.

This is explained in part by Maslow's Pyramid, the
hierarchy of human needs that was identified by the psychologist Abraham Maslow. At the top of the pyramid,
where people would like to be focusing, is our need to be
self-actualized, to realize and integrate our talents, intel-
lect, values, and physical and emotional needs. In the new
work environments, where companies are offering to empower employees, self-actualization is being promoted.

At the bottom of the pyramid, Maslow put physical security, the need everyone has to feel safe from danger, harm, or risk. In the new competitive environment, this kind of security is exactly what management cannot offer. With heightened competition, downsizings, and new demands from customers, there is virtually no job security.

In effect, then, managers are sending their employees conflicting messages. On the one hand, they are encouraging them to go for the top of Maslow's Pyramid, to realize their greatest aspirations. On the other hand, managers are telling their employees that their most basic needs for safety and security are not guaranteed. No wonder, in such a climate, that trust becomes a critical issue.

Trust in a time of change is based on two things: predictability and capability. In any organization, people want to know what to expect; they want predictability. That's why, in the middle of change, trust is eroded when the ground rules change. This is particularly true in large, previously successful corporations. Under the old psychological contract between the company and its employees, predictability consisted of an implicit agreement: in return for years of service, tenure, and loyalty, the employees could count on employment. The career path was also predictable. For example, an engineer knew that his or her work life would progress with a certain regularity, starting by working on a small project, then a larger project, leading to an assignment as an assistant manager, then on to being a manager. There was a map that people could follow to rise within the organization. With layoffs and downsizing, the old contract has been broken. Not only is the guaranteed career path gone, but so is the guarantee of employment.

In this new context, people are still looking for predictability. But predictability has to take a different form
and apply to different situations. Predictability consists
of intention and ground rules: what are our general goals
and how will we make decisions? The more leaders clarify the company's intentions and ground rules, the more
people will be able to predict and influence what happens to them—even in the middle of a constantly shift-
ing situation.

An example of a manager establishing predictability
occurred at a large electronics company when the head
of a division announced his determination to adopt a
new style of management. At the start of the program,
he talked with all the managers and supervisors to
explain the new direction. He told them, "If you believe
you cannot manage in this new way, and you come and
tell me, I will find a useful job for you somewhere in the
company. But if I discover that you aren't managing
within the new plan, there's no such guarantee."

When he started the program, one or two people
came forward to say they couldn't manage in the new
style, and he found them new jobs. Several others didn't
come forward but were identified as nonperformers. As
promised, he got rid of them. Then, one year later, the
division head spoke to the group again. This time, he
said, "We've been at it for a year. Now everyone knows
what we're talking about, and we're starting to gain
momentum. Because we have some responsibility for
your being the kind of manager you are, and we have
changed the rules in the middle of your career, I'm going
to reissue my invitation. If you don't think you can manage in this new way, come and see me."

As a result of this second invitation, more people
came forward. The program picked up even more

momentum, and managers and employees felt that they understood both the company's intentions and its ground rules for creating change.

The second part of the equation is capability. To trust an organization, both managers and their reports must define the capability that each is providing; and each side has to believe that the other is capable of playing the new role. In the old organization, capability was defined in terms of deliverables. Bosses would say, "I don't care how you get it done; just produce the results I want." Now managers realize that if their processes are aligned and in control, the desired results will follow. To make this happen, managers and employees must identify needed capabilities and negotiate the roles and responsibilities of those involved in the process before each will trust the situation.

Rather than just checking on milestones and timetables, managers should ask how the work will get done. They may occasionally attend cross-functional team meetings to listen to the participants talk about how the project is going, or they may talk with others across the different functions to get feedback on the project. And, by the same token, those undertaking the project may want to negotiate with the manager or others to access

How the team performs, whether or not it wins, and what the future holds is as much in the hands of employees as leaders.

different capabilities, perspectives, and experiences. When each side understands the needs, capabilities, and objectives of the other, trust can be built.

One of the consequences of this new approach is a shift to interdependency. Employees are no longer dependent on the company in a hierarchical relationship. Now the company and its employees are interdependent; and the employees themselves are interdependent. In essence, the company is creating a new team and offering its people a fair shot at playing on the team. How the team performs, whether or not it wins, and what the future holds is as much in the hands of the players as the leaders. The only real security the company has to offer is a chance for people to work together to create the future and to achieve their goals.

A n organization, like a mobile, is a web of interconnections; a change in one area throws a different part off balance. Managing these ripple effects is what makes managing change a dynamic proposition with unexpected challenges.

Consider, for example, what typically happens when companies undertake process reengineering. For the sake of simplicity, let's consider the best of circumstances. The cross-functional team has met its objectives for cutting cycle time and costs while increasing productivity and customer satisfaction. Functional chimneys are turning into pipelines. Wasted time and unnecessary activities are a thing of the past. Decisions are based on what's best for the overall business. The pilot projects proved it can work; the executive champions are thrilled; it looks like it's time to institutionalize the new process. Teams that get this far should be both commended and forewarned.

Getting through the pilot stage of a change program is a long way from a companywide scale-up. A "not-invented-here" mentality is often more intense within companies than it is with outsiders. But the issues surrounding process reengineering are not just a matter of internal competition; they involve a complex set of questions that affect systems as well as individuals.

Functional managers find themselves wondering, "What happens to me now? Is there a job for me? Is it one I want? How do I prove my value in this new environment?" People who are accustomed to managing budgets, allocating resources, and being actively involved in projects are likely to take a dim view of redesigned processes that give cross-functional teams the decision-making authority they had previously enjoyed. The transition from being a hands-on leader to a talent broker is not easy.

Meanwhile, team members have questions of their own: "If we take all the risks, what are the rewards? What happens when the project is over? What does my career path look like if I go in and out of a functional organization depending on which project I'm working on?" Evaluation, compensation, and career development all need to be redesigned in light of new process requirements. If they are not, there is little incentive for individuals to use the new processes even if they do work.

Human resources is not the only support system that must be reevaluated. The organizational mobile has many dimensions—culture, strategy, education, information systems, technology—and they all need to hang together. If the parts of the organizational system are not considered in concert, they will inevitably clash. In the case of process redesign, when the entire mobile is not balanced, reengineering is reduced to a mapping exercise.

M ANAGING CHANGE MEANS balancing the mobile; the question is how to do it. One way is to depend on managers scattered throughout the organization to have a shared awareness of how the various parts need to interact and for everyone to trust that this general perception will ultimately pull the organization together. Of course, that's assuming an awful lot. Another option that has worked well in a number of companies is a Transition Management Team.

What the TMT is not is as important as what it is. It is not a new layer of bureaucracy or a permanent job for fading executives. It is not a steering committee, which is usually a body that convenes periodically to guide those who are actually doing the work of the organization.

The TMT oversees the large-scale corporate change effort; it makes sure that all the change initiatives fit together. It is made up of 8 to 12 highly talented leaders who commit all their time to making the transition a reality. The team members and what they are trying to accomplish must be accepted by the power structure of the organization. For the duration of the change process, they are the CEO's version of the national guard. The CEO should be able to say, "I can sleep well tonight; the transition team is managing this."

A Transition Management Team is not a new layer of bureaucracy or a job for fading executives.

The CEO's job is to be a visible champion for the transformation, articulating the context and rationale for the new corporate direction. Working out the guidelines and ensuring that they are understood and used is the TMT's task. This means that the team captain is essentially the transition COO. As such, he or she must have proven talent and credibility, understand the long-term vision of the company, have a complete knowledge of the business, and have the confidence of the CEO.

When the change process has stabilized and moved to a phase of continuous improvement, the TMT disbands. Until then, the team has the overall responsibility for the transition. It reports to the CEO regularly, but the CEO doesn't run the team on a day-to-day basis. The TMT has funding authority, the power to stop projects that are out of sync with the overall direction of the change effort, and input into evaluations of projects and the individuals or teams who perform them.

In addition to the overall captain, the TMT must include a person who pays particular attention to the emotional and behavioral issues raised by change, making sure that they are neither ignored nor compromised; team captains of the major initiatives, such as information technology, process redesign, and compensation; and the team captains of human resources and communications. All teams, including the human resources and communications teams, are cross-functional and drawn from different levels in the organization.

The TMT manages the operational issues of the change effort. In addition, it needs to anticipate and manage the reactions, questions, and concerns that change generates. The TMT must be sure that the coordination and communication are congruent and ample. Ideally, the TMT captain could oversee all these elements, making sure that the operational pieces fit together and that the emotional issues are addressed openly and clearly. But practical experience suggests that in most large change programs, the emotional issues are likely to get short shrift. In setting up a TMT, companies should adopt a fail-safe approach: create a position to oversee the emotional and behavioral issues unless you can prove with confidence that you don't need one. The point is not to make operational changes hostage to some emotional ideal; the point is to acknowledge the importance of the emotional issues and to recognize that unless someone owns an issue, no one is responsible for it.

For that reason, creating the position of a guide can be an important safeguard. While the TMT captain and the captains of the cross-functional teams are still responsible for identifying and addressing the emotional and behavioral issues that they see emerging, the guide makes sure that these issues are identified and discussed. This individual must not only understand the business but also be sensitive to people issues and be both well respected and well connected within the organization. He or she must think strategically about the transformation that the company must undergo and the underlying beliefs, behaviors, skills, and support systems that will be necessary to make it happen. For example, if the company has always thought of itself as an engineering-driven, product-focused organization, and the early strategy work makes clear that the company must become a customer-focused service organization, the responsibility of the guide is to ensure that the TMT carries this paradigm shift deep into the organization.

Most corporate change efforts are fundamentally about moving information across old and obsolete boundaries.

The TMT has eight primary responsibilities. This team is not, however, solely accountable for fulfilling these tasks.

Establish context for change and provide guidance. The CEO and other executives establish the company's strategic vision. The TMT makes sure that everyone in the organization shares a common understanding of that vision and understands the company's competitive situation. By organizing discussions throughout the organization, the TMT spreads the company's vision and competitive situation so that individuals and teams can accurately align their own activities with the company's new overall direction.

Stimulate conversation. Most older, larger companies have formalized their operations in such functional isolation that conversations across levels or functions rarely take place. Instead, people have grown accustomed to presentations followed by inquisitions. Moreover, when resources are scarce and time pressures are severe, conversation often seems a luxury. Yet most change efforts are fundamentally about moving information across old and obsolete boundaries. Consequently, organizing early conversations between different parts of the company and making those conversations an important, sanctioned part of the change process is a critical task for the TMT. Early, open-ended conversations often result in the most productive outcomes; conversely, project leaders who press for early results and close off conversation inside the company usually get to the end of a project with little to show in the way of new insight or real breakthrough thinking.

Provide appropriate resources. The TMT has two types of significant power: the power to allocate resources to make things happen and the power to kill projects that are no longer needed. In the first category, the TMT does command time and budgets. Frequently, change efforts falter because the people who are drafted to play important roles in leading teams work only on the margins. As a result, the team never has a real process owner or receives adequate attention. The TMT can change that; it can designate individuals who take on the authority and are given the time and resources to do the job properly.

The TMT can also kill off old projects that no longer have a high priority. In many organizations, the operating maxim is, "Old projects never die, they just get under-funded." Nobody is willing to make the tough decision to cut a project that has outlived its usefulness. The result is a lot of projects that are more dead than alive but still dis-tracting people and using resources. The TMT needs to be the tough-minded terminator of these projects.

Coordinate and align projects. As company's shift into fast-paced change programs, task forces, teams, and projects proliferate. One result is a great deal of enthusi-asm, energy, and activity. Another is confusion. Even if every activity is valid and necessary, the problem is that they don't seem to fit together. The TMT has two tasks: coordinating and aligning the projects into building blocks that fit together; and communicating to the whole organization how the pieces align so that others can see the larger picture and appreciate that there is a coherent plan.

Ensure congruence of messages, activities, poli-cies, and behaviors. One of the major complaints of people in organizations undergoing a transition is that management doesn't "walk the talk." They say "empow-erment"—and then shoot down every new idea that comes from their employees. The TMT's job is to be on the lookout for inconsistencies that undermine the cred-ibility of the change effort. The message, the measures, the behaviors, and the rewards must match.

Provide opportunities for joint creation. Most change programs today embrace the concept of empow-erment but never get around to defining it. In some companies, empowerment essentially is, "Do what I say and act as if you like it." In others, it is interpreted to mean, "Everybody gets to vote on everything." My working definition of empowerment is a true opportunity for employees throughout the company to create the future together. That means ensuring that all employees, whether managers, directors, factory workers, or technical staff, have the information they need to make correct decisions and take appropriate actions. Clearly, the TMT cannot do all the communicating and teaching; it is the designer, coordinator, and support source for that learning and creation.

Anticipate, identify, and address people problems. There is a reason why the guide and the communications and human resources teams are all represented on the TMT: people issues are at the heart of change. For example, a change that involves delayering, changing job descriptions, or compensation also requires advance notification and long lead time. Communications and human resources are critical to success, yet there are routine shortages of talent, diversity of perspective, dollars, and share of mind. Cross-functional teams in communications and human resources represent an opportunity for gathering and distributing information, both horizontally and vertically, throughout the organization.

Prepare the critical mass. Given the complexity of scale-up from creating the pilot to making it the norm, it is important to design into the work from the very beginning the resources and strategy necessary for replication and learning transfer. Most teams will need guidance on how to do this as well as help to make sure that what they are doing fits with other activities.

The organizing element of all these activities is the hard work of educating, training, and preparing the organization to think, feel, and act differently. In companies where change is successful, the leaders look at the whole mobile and the congruence of operations and emotions. It is far too easy to equate change with specific tasks. When the TMT manages both the content and the process, the operations and the emotions, it provides a powerful lever for change.

The real contribution of leadership in a time of change lies in managing the dynamics, not the pieces. The fundamental job of leadership is to deal with the dynamics of change, the confluence and congruence of the forces that change unleashes, so that the company is better prepared to compete.

Originally published in November–December 1993
Reprint 93602

The Reinvention Roller Coaster

Risking the Present for a
Powerful Future

TRACY GOSS,

RICHARD PASCALE, AND

ANTHONY ATHOS

Executive Summary

BY NOW, EVERY CEO KNOWS how to create cross–
functional teams, reduce defects, and redesign business
processes to lower costs and improve performance. But
all too often, activities like these offer nothing more than
incremental change. Managers looking for a more fundamental shift in their organizations' capabilities do not
need to improve themselves; they need to reinvent themselves.

Reinvention is not changing what is, but creating
what isn't. When British Airways declared itself the
world's favorite airline, it faced the challenge of becoming a different company, not just a better one. When
Europcar decided to become the most efficient rental-
car company in Europe and Häagen-Dazs chose to
make a visit to its European shops an exciting event,

they didn't just need to focus on *doing* things to improve their competitiveness.

When a company sets out on the journey of reinvention, it must uncover and then alter the invisible assumptions and premises on which its decisions and actions are based. This organization *context* is the sum of the past and dictates what is possible for the future. When managers reinvent themselves and their companies, they create a new context that leads everyone to embrace a seemingly impossible future.

The hard work of reinvention includes assembling a critical mass of stakeholders to do an organizational audit, create urgency, harness contention, and engineer breakdowns that reveal weak spots. An organization must confront its most life-threatening problems to summon the courage to abandon what is for what might be.

Kodak, IBM, AMERICAN EXPRESS, AND GENERAL MOTORS have recently sacked their CEOs. All were capable executives with impressive track records. All had promised turnarounds, and all had spearheaded downsizing, delayering, and reengineering programs in vigorous efforts to deliver those promises. Indeed, most of these efforts lowered costs, increased productivity, and improved profitability—at least for a while. Yet despite this frenzy of activity, the competitive vitality of these companies continued to ebb away until finally their boards felt compelled to act.

What went wrong? The simplistic answer is "leadership." All these boards wound up blaming their CEOs for poor leadership and inadequate strategic vision. But press the members of those boards—or the shaken executives—for a better answer, and you will uncover uncertainty, bafflement, even an occasional muddled insight that the answer lies somewhere deeper than any board or executive is equipped to look.

These experienced businesspeople see the problem as "leadership" because they see the solution as "change." And surely, they tell themselves, any leader deserving of that name can successfully implement change. They are right. With all the practice of the 1980s, every CEO knows how to create cross-functional teams, reduce defects, and redesign business processes in ways that lower costs and improve performance. A CEO who cannot set ambitious new goals and does not know how to try harder to reach them deserves the boot.

Incremental change isn't enough for many companies today. They don't need to change what is; they need to create what isn't.

But what these CEOs are missing is that such incremental change is not enough for many companies today. Managers groping about for a more fundamental shift in their organizations' capabilities must realize that change programs treat symptoms, not underlying conditions. These companies do not need to improve themselves; they need to reinvent themselves.

Reinvention is not changing what is, but creating what isn't. A butterfly is not more caterpillar or a better or improved caterpillar; a butterfly is a different creature. Leaders of three multinational companies with whom we have worked have grappled with this distinction. When British Airways declared itself the world's favorite airline in the 1980s, it faced the challenge of becoming a different company, not just a better company. The same held true when Europcar decided to become the most user friendly and efficient rental-car company in Europe and not just an omnipresent one. And when Häagen-Dazs chose to make a visit to its European ice-cream shops an exciting event, the company didn't need just to change what it did or how work got done.

When a company reinvents itself, it must alter the underlying assumptions and invisible premises on which its decisions and actions are based. This *context* is the sum of all the conclusions that members of the organization have reached. It is the product of their experience and their interpretations of the past, and it determines the organization's social behavior, or culture. Unspoken and even unacknowledged conclusions about the past dictate what is possible for the future.

To reinvent itself, an organization must first uncover its hidden context. Only when an organization is threatened, losing momentum, or eager to break new ground will it confront its past and begin to understand why it must break with its outmoded present. And only then will a company's employees come to believe in a powerful new future, a future that may seem beyond the organization's reach. Admittedly, the notion that companies should "stretch" themselves to achieve unprecedented goals is not new. But executives have frequently underestimated the wrenching shift—the internal conflict and soul-searching–that goes hand in hand with a break from the present way of thinking and operating. And because executives have not understood this as they announced their grandiose "strategic intentions," employees have often ignored the call to arms.

Unless managers orchestrate the creation of a new context, all that the organizations are *doing* to improve their competitiveness—whether they are improving service, accelerating product development, or increasing the flexibility of manufacturing—will at worst yield unproductive churnings and at best produce meaningful but episodic change.

But if a company authentically reinvents itself, if it alters its context, it not only has the means to alter its culture and achieve unprecedented results in quality, service ratings, cycle time, market share, and, finally, financial performance; it also will have the ability to sustain these improvements regardless of any changes in the business environment.

One company that nearly succeeded in reinventing itself is the Ford Motor Company. From 1980 through 1982, Ford lost $3 billion. By 1986, its earnings surpassed those of much larger General Motors for the first time since the 1920s. By 1988, Ford's profits reached $5.3 billion, and return on stockholders' equity hit 26.3%. Its market share in the United States had increased five points to 22%. Cycle time for the development of an automobile decreased from eight years to five. Quality, according to J.D. Power surveys, jumped from the bottom 25% to the top 10% of all automobiles that were sold in the United States. And surveys and focus groups of both union and salaried employees recorded dramatic shifts in their perceptions of management, morale, and company loyalty.

The journey to reinvent yourself and your company is a sink-or-swim proposition.

The key to these remarkable improvements? Employees consistently reported that Ford had somehow become an entirely different company than it had been five years earlier. Ford had left behind its past as a

rigidly hierarchical company driven by financial considerations to pursue a future in which a concern for quality and new products became the overriding priority.

Ford's organizational reinvention proved to be successful. But unfortunately, the company's leaders at the
time were not similarly reinvented, as their failure to
invest sufficiently in the core business revealed. Sustaining the company's momentum in the 1990s, therefore, has become a challenging task.

Creating a New Context

Most executives who have any inkling of what reinvention entails flinch at the prospect of taking on this 500-
pound gorilla. "The journey to reinvent yourself and
your company is not as scary as they say it is; it's worse,"
says Mort Meyerson, chairman of Perot Systems, an
information-systems company that is assisting in many
corporate reinventions. "You step into the abyss out of
the conviction that the only way to compete in the long
haul is to be a totally different company. It's a sink-or-
swim proposition."

It should come as no surprise, then, that many CEOs
end up sinking. After creating a context or being the
product of one, they either don't have the courage—or
see the need—to throw it away. But in defense of these
CEOs, it is easy to look for the root cause of declining
competitiveness and not see it.

Consider this analogy. You inherit your grand-
mother's house. Unknown to you is one peculiarity: all
the light fixtures have bulbs that give off blue rather
than yellow light. You find that you don't like the feel of
the rooms and spend a lot of time and money repainting
walls, reupholstering furniture, and replacing carpets.

You never seem to get it quite right, but nonetheless, you rationalize that at least it is improving with each thing you do. Then one day you notice the blue lightbulbs and change them. Suddenly, all that you fixed is broken. Context is like the color of the light, not the objects in the room. Context colors everything in the corporation. More accurately, the context alters what we see, usually without our being aware of it.

Many CEOs don't have the courage, or see the need, to throw away the context they've created.

Much-abused IBM is an example of a company that has been doing things to the objects in the room without changing the color of the light. IBM was among the vanguard in employing most contemporary business techniques, such as pursuing Six Sigma quality (3.4 defects per one million units), empowerment, delayering, and downsizing. But because IBM failed to alter its context—the "IBM way" of controlling and predicting every aspect of the business—these change programs did not serve as steps to a powerful future.

The company leaders sought to instill an entrepreneurial spirit that would lead employees to take bold initiatives with new product ideas and with customers. But the context in which they managed made entrepreneurship at IBM an oxymoron. That context—ever-positive and upbeat—demanded that managers demonstrate how a course of action would play out five steps into the future before they could take step one. This left managers unwilling to risk, let alone abandon, what the company had become for what it might be.

At the other end of the spectrum is Motorola, a familiar example of successful reinvention. Over the course of its 65-year history, Motorola has on several occasions decided that a new future was at hand, first in car radios, then in television, consumer electronics, and semiconductors, and recently in microcomputers, cellular phones, and pagers. Each shift has been marked by fundamentally altering the kind of company that Motorola was in order to compete in entirely different industries. This involved self-imposed upheaval: selling off successful but older businesses and taking big gambles on the new ones.

In facing these challenges, Motorola's leaders realized the importance of context. Motorola was once a collection of fiefdoms dominated by macho engineers who mistakenly thought that they had no serious rivals. But in the late 1970s, CEO Robert Galvin recognized that the inward-looking company was not prepared to face intensifying Japanese competition.

He forced everyone to confront quality problems, divisional limitations, and the Japanese threat. To do so, the company had to become self-questioning, outward looking, and much more humble. A healthy degree of self-criticism replaced the former sense of superiority. In 1989, one year before he stepped down as CEO, Galvin challenged Motorola to become "the world's premier company," a guiding vision that transcended the company's former definition of itself as the best maker of its products.

"The world's premier company" seems too vague to inspire a powerful new future, but as Motorola's employees began to come to terms with the idea, they were spurred by the challenge of being the best in every facet of their business. The vision served as a reminder that the company must constantly challenge its sense of what is possible in order to resist the downward pull of habit and routine.

The Doing Trap

Author Rita Mae Brown defines insanity as doing the same thing again and again but expecting different results. With no awareness of the power of context, we continue to beat our heads against the same wall.

What are we missing? This parallel may help. Scientists at the turn of the century treated time as a constant, a given. But physicists studying light (photons) found increasing experimental evidence that something was amiss. They held fast, however, to the ether-wave theory of light and its central premise that the speed of light was a variable. When Einstein speculated that the speed of light might be a constant, he was drawn to look elsewhere for a variable that could account for the elasticity of the cosmos. Time was the only candidate. Einstein created an intellectual puzzle that

With no awareness of the power of context, we continue to beat our heads against the same wall.

forced him to look "outside the box." His consideration of a new possibility launched him on the intellectual odyssey that led to the Special and General Theories of Relativity and revolutionized the world of physics. He created a new context for looking at the universe.

Like time to turn-of-the-century physicists, *doing* is the assumed managerial constant. To manage is to *do* something; managers are selected and promoted based on their ability to get things done. But what if something else is the constant, and doing is the variable?

Like Einstein's thought experiment of riding on a photon of light to see what the world looked like from that perspective, the executive who would master reinvention must journey into a largely unfamiliar and uncomfortable territory, the territory of *being*.[1] Being alters action; context shapes thinking and perception. When you fundamentally alter the context, the foundation on which people construct their understanding of the world, actions are altered accordingly.

Context sets the stage; being pertains to whether the actor lives the part or merely goes through the motions. Organizations and the people in them are being something all the time. On occasion, we describe them as "conservative," or "hard charging," or "resistant to change." Trouble is, aside from such casual generalizations, we concentrate mostly on what we are doing and let being fend for itself.

That may be because we Westerners have few mental hooks or even words for excursions into being. The Japanese chart the journey across life in terms of perfecting one's inner nature, or being. They call it *kokoro*.[2] In contrast, Westerners typically assess their progression through adulthood in terms of personal wealth or levels of accomplishments. To the Japanese, merely *doing* these things is meaningless unless one is able to become deeper and wiser along the way.

Many Western CEOs will undoubtedly say that all this smacks of something philosophical or, far worse, theological and therefore has presumably little relevance for managers. But an organization's being determines its context, its possibilities. Remarkable shifts in context can happen only when there is a shift in being. Since IBM's would-be entrepreneurs continued to act "appropriately" and "conservatively," it is hardly surprising that the context of risk taking that former Chairman and CEO John Akers tried to create never took hold.

Our difficulty in discerning what a business is explains why so many efforts at corporate revitalization have failed. Consider all the retail chains throughout the country, including Saks and Macy's, that have tried to counter or capture Nordstrom's magic but with little success. Nordstrom's way of being has enabled it to win in seemingly impossible circumstances. For example, it was able to launch a successful expansion program in the Northeastern United States when that region was gripped by deep recession. That expansion helped Nordstrom become the leading department store chain in the country in terms of sales per square foot. Nordstrom now has 64 stores, annual sales of $2.89 billion, and an annual growth rate of 20%.

While the other chains can copy some of what Nordstrom is doing, they don't seem to realize that Nordstrom is living its motto, "Respond to Unreasonable Customer Requests." This way of being leads employees to relish the challenges that customers toss at them. Usually, meeting these demands entails little more than providing just a bit more service. But occasionally it means hand delivering items purchased by phone to the airport for a customer

Nordstrom encourages salespeople to respond to demanding customers by keeping scrapbooks of "heroic" acts and paying on commission.

with a last-minute business trip, changing a customer's flat tire, or paying a customer's parking ticket when in-store gift wrapping has taken longer than expected.

Nordstrom encourages these acts by promoting its best employees, keeping scrapbooks of "heroic" acts, and paying its salespeople entirely on commission, through which they usually earn about twice what they would at a rival's store. For go-getters who really love to sell,

Nordstrom is nirvana. But the system weeds out those who can't meet such demanding standards and selects those prepared to be what Nordstrom stands for.

Rivals scrambling to keep up have instituted in-house charm schools and issued vision statements trumpeting the importance of customers and the value of service. They have copied Nordstrom by introducing commissions and incentives. They have loosened their refund policies. Without exception, these actions have failed to close the gap. The problem seems to be an understanding of what it means to respond to unreasonable customer demands. To many salespeople at competing stores, it means that the customer comes first—within reason. Customer demands must be met—unless these demands are ridiculous. But at Nordstrom, each ridiculous customer request is an opportunity for a "heroic" act by an employee, an opportunity to expand on the store's reputation. To compete with Nordstrom, other stores must shift "who they are" in relation to the customer, not just what they do for the customer.

Shifts in being are not merely upbeat intellectual "ah-ha's." "Oh my God" is more likely to be uttered than "Eureka." The acid test of such a shift is whether or not it is intellectually and emotionally jolting. Executives at Europcar, the second largest rental-car company in Europe, understand this phenomenon.

Europcar's country fiefdoms maintained separate operating systems that could not deal with the increasing number of cross-border travelers.

In January 1992, CEO Fredy Dellis surveyed the competitive situation and did not like what he saw. While revenues were rising slowly, profits were plummeting.

He estimated that it cost Europcar $13 to process each rental agreement (mostly by hand), compared with $1 at Hertz and Avis. Past attempts at incremental improvement had failed to close this gap. Much of the problem seemed to stem from the company's structure. Europcar had been built through acquisitions and was a loose federation of rental-car companies throughout Europe, each of which was convinced it knew its country best. Worse still, each country fiefdom built and maintained its own operating system, and these incompatible systems could not deal with the increasing number of cross-border travelers. Europcar was a parochial, balkanized organization whose country managers were preoccupied with protecting their national idiosyncrasies and their turf.

Dellis's response was to initiate the Greenway Project, a plan to revamp Europcar's entire operating system—how reservations were made, how rental operations flowed from check-out to check-in, the financially critical activities of fleet purchasing and fleet utilization. But a companywide operating system would drastically change the way the country units did business and would thus threaten their distinct national identities. Bickering between country managers and the design team, whose members themselves were drawn from the separate country operations, threatened the entire project.

But in early 1993, a small miracle happened when the 35 top managers and the design team gathered in Nice, France. The design team had been invited to demonstrate the new system, on which they had made enormous headway with very little input or encouragement from their senior sponsors. But these top managers, finally recognizing the importance of Greenway for lowering Europcar's cost structure to competitors' levels, took on the task of bridging this gulf of distrust and misunderstanding.

As these managers moved through the design team's presentations on the components of the operating system and what it could accomplish in terms of cost reduction and improved service and fleet utilization, the discussion grew animated with much give-and-take. Participants say the disbelief and alienation felt by both designers and senior managers was transformed into growing excitement about the new possibilities for the flow of information throughout the company. Moreover, by uniting all the operations, the whole would become much more formidable than the previous collection of individual parts. The antagonism that had marked relationships between parts of the company began to fade; everyone at the gathering began to behave like part of a team. The shift for Europcar toward becoming a company that could coalesce across geographical borders and through levels of hierarchy to become an innovator in its field was well under way.

Inventing a Powerful Future

Statements of vision from chief executives have bewildered and even amused employees who just don't get why a CEO would describe a future that their experience says can never materialize. The ensuing action plans are built inevitably on company notions about how things *really* work around here and employees' experience of the last change effort. It all adds up to pulling the leaden past toward a future we never seem to reach.[3]

As we have said, reinvention entails creating a new possibility for the future, one that past experiences and current predictions would indicate is impossible. Sir

Colin Marshall did this by declaring that British Airways would be the "world's favorite airline" when it ranked among the worst. Before its turnaround in the 1980s, the airline's frequent maintenance-related delays, poor food, and Aeroflot-like standards of service had inspired long-suffering customers to say that its initials actually stood for "bloody awful."

A declaration from a leader generates an essential element of reinvention. It creates the possibility of a new future that evokes widespread interest and commitment. When a declaration is well stated, it is always visually imaginable (putting a man on the moon) or exceptionally simple (becoming the world's favorite airline). The declaration becomes the magnetic North, the focal point. By contrast, a vision provides a more elaborate description of the desired state and the criteria against which success will be measured.

A declaration forces you to stand in the new future, undertaking a series of steps not in order to be the world's favorite airline *someday*, but to be that airline *now*. Sir Colin began leading British Airways down that road by going to those who dealt closely with customers and asking them what needed to happen. The answers included everything from making sure that the concourse lights were always on to seeing that meals on short flights were easy to deliver and unwrap. Being the best in customers' eyes also meant putting the airline's operations under the marketing department, so that instead of moving people as if they were packages, all operating decisions would start from a concern for the passenger. Today British Airways's service ranks among the best, and it is one of the most profitable airlines in the world.

But what happens when a company reaches its future? Where does it go from there? This was the situation

Häagen-Dazs faced after its stunning success in exporting its "Dedicated to Pleasure" brand identity to the European market in 1989. A team of young, hard-charging recruits from the world's leading food-products companies had thought it would take anywhere from three to five years to gain a presence in a market where competitors ranged from giants like Mars and Nestlé to thousands of home recipe boutiques. Against the odds, this team launched the brand in June 1989, with a daring ad campaign featuring scantily clad couples indulging in the pleasures of ice cream. Within 18 months, Häagen-Dazs was the leading dairy ice cream in Western Europe. The team had pulled off one of the most successful new product launches the packaged food industry had ever seen.

Then an interesting thing began to happen. Once victory was achieved, bureaucracy took over. Paris headquarters began to quarrel with country management teams. Marketing began to flex its muscles at the expense of sales and shops operations. Headquarters in the United States was too worried about Ben & Jerry's encroachments to notice. The young hotshots in Europe began to wonder how to protect their position and, more important, what they could do for an encore.

John Riccitiello, general manager of Häagen-Dazs International, concluded that his organization had already used up its future; incremental improvements, he realized, could not restore momentum. He toyed with embracing the ambitious goal of making Häagen-Dazs Europe's leading premium food brand. But this goal seemed compelling only to top managers, not to everyone in the company.

Häagen-Dazs built a future by deciding that a visit to its shops would be a memorable event for customers and staff.

Riccitiello decided to shift the context of "beating the competition, being the best" and a strategy of selling pleasure to a new context of "celebrating the experience of being alive." He believed that there would be more longevity in a future of selling excitement and pizzazz. A visit to a Häagen-Dazs shop, he determined, would be a memorable event for customers.

This new future generated an important shift in the company's recruitment policy. Interviews with job candidates are now treated much like theatrical auditions. "We aren't just looking for people to clear tables and dispense ice cream," Riccitiello says. "So when a group of prospects come in, we give them impromptu situations and see what they do. Do they ad-lib? Do they freeze and look to others for the right answer? We ask them to juggle four ice-cream cones. We want our shops to be an event, a place where customers and staff celebrate the experience of something that tastes great and gives you—even if just for a moment—a sense that it's worth being alive. It became our mission to provide that feeling."

To that end, the company created a senior position. This "Director of Magic," as the woman given the job has been dubbed, works with shop managers and scoopers to help them generate ideas that make them look forward to their work. When coming to a Häagen-Dazs shop becomes an exciting event for staff and customers, the competition has a hard time measuring up.

Executive Reinvention

During our 35 years of research, writing, teaching, and consulting for U.S., European, and Japanese corporations, we have found, particularly in senior executives, an unwillingness to think rigorously and patiently about themselves or their ideas. We often find senior executives perched like a threatened aristocracy, entitled, aloof, and sensing doom. Flurries of restructuring or downsizing are like the desperate attempts of uncomprehending heirs who try to slow the decline of the family estate. Each successive reaction is misconstrued as bold action to "set things right."

When leading an organization into the future, executives come to a fork in the road. As they come face-to-face with their organizations' needs to reinvent themselves, many executives hope for the best and opt for the prudent path of change. Even when they choose reinvention, their feet get cold. Thrown into the unfamiliar territory of reinvention, where the steps along the path and the outcomes themselves are often unpredictable, the responsible thing to do, many executives think, is to get things back on track. It is not surprising that so many senior executives decline invitations to reinvent themselves and their companies. It is like aging: experts tell us that it is difficult, yet most of us hope to go through it without pain.

There is another choice, but it requires executive reinvention, a serious inquiry into oneself as a leader. This is not a psychological process to fix something that's wrong, but an inquiry that reveals the context from which an executive makes decisions. People have contexts just as organizations do. Our individual context is our hidden strategy for dealing with life; it determines all the choices we make. On the surface, our context is our formula for winning, the source of our success. But on closer examination, this context is the box within which a person operates and determines what is possible and impossible for him or her as a leader and, by extension, for the organization.

A good example is a CEO who wanted to increase the

One CEO worked hard to make his company grow, but he opposed every expansion.

annual revenues of his family-run manufacturing business from $80 million to $200 million within five years. He had been working very hard toward this goal for a number of years and was dissatisfied with the slow progress.

But when people proposed expansion plans, like adding a new product line or entering a new market, all he could see were the incredible problems: the outside executives that would have to be brought on board, the new expertise that existing managers, including complacent family members, would have to acquire, and so on. He refused to endorse such plans, or if he did let a plan go forward, he would halt it whenever contention arose.

If you had asked him how he had spent his day, he would say, "I spent it working on the growth of the company." But when he finally stopped to examine what was going wrong, he realized that he was operating from a context of avoiding conflict, which was inconsistent with a commitment to ambitious growth. He understood that this was why all the things he was doing to expand the business were not working.

He could then put a clear choice before the family board: either they pursue becoming a $200 million company with their eyes open to the fact that there would be chaos, conflict, and upheaval, or they settle for incremental growth. The board decided on the latter (sales of $100 million). They left achieving the larger future to the next generation.

Managing the Present from the Future

An organization that has a clear grasp of its own assumptions about the past is often motivated to alter the context in which the company is embedded. This in turn requires a shift in the organization's being and a powerful vision of the future. The activities involved in reinventing an organization require persistence and flexibility. Some extend over the entire effort, and others are steps along the way.

1. Assembling a Critical Mass of Key Stakeholders. Leading pilgrims on the journey of reinventing an organization should never be left to the top eight or ten executives. It is deceptively easy to generate consensus among this group; they usually are a tight fraternity, and it is difficult to spark deep self-examination among them. If there are revelations, they may never extend beyond this circle.

The group leading reinvention should include critical but seldom-seen people like key technologists or engineers.

As proven by the experiences of such companies as Ford, British Petroleum, Chase Bank, AT&T, Europcar, Thomas Cook, and Häagen-Dazs, this group must encompass a critical mass of stakeholders—the employees "who really make things happen around here." Some hold sway over key resources. Others are central to informal opinion networks. The group may often include critical but seldom-seen people like key technologists and leading process engineers. The goal is a flywheel effect, where enough key players get involved and enrolled that it creates a momentum to carry the process forward.

These key stakeholders first must determine if their company has what it takes to remain competitive and, if not, what to do about it. In the process, such a group will typically put unspoken grievances and suspicions on the table. Its members will learn to work together and to respect nonconforming opinions. All this constitutes a shift in the way participants are being, from a relationship of distrust and resignation toward an authentic, powerful partnership. This is not easy, nor is it enough. But it is a beginning.

Once such a shift has taken place, actions and reactions that previously could not have occurred happen quite naturally, and with surprising results.

Such a watershed event occurred during Ford's transformation in the 1980s. The upper-level managers in charge of the Engineering Division and the Power Train Division, which designed engines and transmissions, were called into one room. Lou Ross, then senior vice president in charge of factories, got right to the point. "Here's the problem," he said. "For 25 years, Power Train and Engineering have been fighting with each other, hurting productivity and quality. Enough is enough. We don't care how long it takes, but we want you to answer one question: Will engineering report to manufacturing, or manufacturing to engineering?"

Now picture a meeting room eight months later, after countless hostile debates. Many of the same people from the Engineering and Power Train divisions were on their hands and knees, discussing the merits of the various organizational charts that covered the floor. There was a lot of give-and-take. Someone asked with an edge of frustration, "Which of these organizational charts is best?" Another person answered, "Maybe *this* is!" A hush fell over the room. He was call-

ing attention to the way they were behaving as colleagues. The important thing was how they were working together, not finding the "perfect" organizational
structure. It took another month to put an "organization" together that didn't reorganize at all but simply
realigned the flows of communication across the traditional Engineering and Power Train chimneys. The
new relationship and all that flowed from it was one of
the pillars of Ford's turnaround. This broad-based shift
in being is central to understanding how Ford com-
pressed the time needed to develop a new model from
eight years to five and catapulted its product quality
from worst to best.

2. Doing an Organizational Audit. The first task of
the key stakeholders is to reveal and confront the company's true competitive situation. This process will also
reveal the barriers to significant organizational
change—the organization's context. A company cannot
get from "here" to "there" without first knowing where
"here" is any more than it can choose reinvention without knowing where "there" is.

The best approach is through a diagnosis that generates a complete picture of how the organization really
works: What assumptions are we making about our
strategic position and customer needs that may no
longer be valid? Which functional units are most influ-
ential, and will they be as important in the future as they
were in the past? What are the key systems that drive
the business? What are the core competencies or skills
of the enterprise? What are the shared values and
idiosyncrasies that comprise the organization's being? If
explored in-depth, these types of questions generate
responses that, taken together, paint a picture of how
things really work.

Europcar created small groups to conduct such an audit. Each took on a crucial issue, such as the company's competitive position, the current system for renting automobiles and tracking information, and the consequences of the country structure. What emerged was a picture of a highly fragmented organization that had no idea what it meant to work together as a whole. As a result of the audit, these crucial stakeholders recognized that without the Greenway Project, Europcar would not be able to compete in the Pan-European market.

3. Creating Urgency, Discussing the Undiscussable. There is an unspoken code of silence in most corporations that conceals the full extent of a corporation's competitive weaknesses. But a threat that everyone perceives and no one talks about is far more debilitating to a company than a threat that has been clearly revealed. Companies, like people, tend to be at least as sick as their secrets.

A company must confront its most life-threatening problems in order to summon the courage to break with the past and embrace a new future. *The Book of Five Rings*, a guide for Japanese samurai written four centuries ago, prescribes the practice of visualizing death in battle as vividly as possible before the actual battle.

A threat that everyone perceives and no one discusses hurts a company much more than a threat that is clearly revealed.

Having experienced "death" beforehand, there is not a lot left to fear, and the warrior fights with complete abandon. Interesting, isn't it, that in confronting the possible, it becomes less probable.

In a sense, managers of companies whose very existence is at stake are lucky; though being honest about the dire situations to which they contributed is painful, it is relatively easy for these managers to convince employees that there is no alternative to a wrenching shift in who and what they are.

4. Harnessing Contention. There is an obscure law of cybernetics—the law of requisite variety—that postulates that any system must encourage and incorporate variety internally if it is to cope with variety externally. This seems innocuous until you consider how variety shows up in organizations. Usually it takes the form of such behavior as siphoning off scarce resources from mainstream activities for back-channel experiments, disagreeing at meetings, and so forth. Almost all significant norm-breaking opinions or behavior in social systems are synonymous with conflict.

Paradoxically, most organizations suppress contention; many managers, among others, cannot stand to be confronted because they assume they should be "in charge." But control kills invention, learning, and commitment.

Conflict jump-starts the creative process.[4] That is why the group process described earlier included a large number of stakeholders. When you extend participation to those really accountable for critical resources, or who hold entrenched positions, or who have been burned by past change attempts, you guarantee conflicts. But as the group faces and handles difficult issues, there is a shift in how they relate to contention. Participants learn to disagree without being disagreeable.

Emotions often accompany creative tension, and these emotions are not altogether pleasant. At Intel, conflict is blunt, at times brutal. Says one observer: "If you're used to tennis, Intel plays rugby, and you walk away with a lot of bruises. They've created a company that takes direct, hard-hitting disagreement as a sign of fitness. You put it all behind you in the locker room, and it's forgotten by the scrimmage the next day."

On a field trip to Tokyo to assess Intel's competitiveness against Japanese quality and service standards, the top management team of 20 became involved in a fierce argument about the company's approach to the Japanese market. Underlying the finger-pointing were long-smoldering resentments on the part of those representing internal Intel customers who could not get the quality and service they desired from manufacturing. Intel COO Craig Barrett, who then headed manufacturing, was a combative partisan in the melee. As one person who was at the meeting described it: "Four-letter words flew back and forth like ping-pong balls in a Beijing master's tournament."

But two days later, team members sat down, sorted out their differences, and put the actions in motion to help Intel match or surpass its Japanese rivals. Barrett says, "I've got pretty thick skin; it takes a lot to penetrate my strongly held convictions. This kind of hard-hitting session is precisely what we all needed to strip us of our illusions. It made us all realize the games we were playing and how they prevented us from facing Japanese competitive realities."

At Honda, anyone can call for a **waigaya** *session, in which people lay their cards on the table and no topic is out of bounds.*

Contrary to what many Westerners might think about the importance of consensus in Japanese culture, institutionalized conflict is an integral part of Japanese management. At Honda, any employee, however junior, can call for a *waigaya* session. The rules are that people lay their cards on the table and speak directly about problems. Nothing is out of bounds, from supervisory deficiencies on the factory floor to perceived lack of support for a design team. Waigaya legitimizes tension so that learning can take place.

The Japanese have learned to disagree without being disagreeable and to harness conflict in a wide variety of ingenious ways. One of their chief principles of organizational design is redundancy—overlapping charters, business activities, and managerial assignments, duplicative databases, and parallel lines of inquiry.

With our deeply ingrained Western concept of organizations as machines, we are quick to judge such overlaps as inefficient, prime candidates for elimination in the current fervor of business process reengineering. But to the Japanese, redundancy and ambiguity spur tension and encourage frequent dialogue and communication. They also generate internal competition, particularly when parallel paths are pursued in new product development. Honda and Sony often use such techniques, assigning identical tasks to competing teams. Periodic project reviews determine which team gets funded to build the final prototype. Sony's compact disc player was developed in this fashion. The manager in charge handed two teams a block of wood the size of a small paperback book and said, "Build it to fit in this space." He recruited talent from Seiko and Citizen Watch who were familiar with miniaturization and ignorant of the traditional boundaries of audio design. Then he stood back and let them fight it out.

Conflict has its human and organizational costs, but it is also an essential fuel for self-questioning and revitalization. Some Western companies have incorporated conflict into their designs with this trade-off in mind.

One is Nordstrom, where there is a built-in tension between providing excellent customer service and taking the idea to such extremes that it threatens economic viability. And since what takes place between staff and customers is the most important piece of Nordstrom's strategy, there are tensions between department heads and buyers, the traditional stars of retailing. Not surprisingly, Nordstrom employees report high tension levels at work. One executive says, "It's wrong to think of Nordstrom as a happy place. But the tensions yield higher performance."

5. Engineering Organizational Breakdowns. It's clear that reinvention is a rocky path and that there will be many breakdowns along the way: systems that threaten to fall apart, deadlines that can't be met, schisms that seem impossible to mend. But just as contention in an organization can be highly productive, these breakdowns make it possible for organizations and individuals to take a hard look themselves and confront the work of reinvention. When an organization sets out to reinvent itself, breakdowns should happen by design rather than by accident.

We might seem to be proposing the willy-nilly seeding of conflict and chaos. Nothing could be further from the truth. Inventing a seemingly impossible future and then managing from that future entails creating concrete tasks that will inevitably lead to breakdowns. These tasks must be carefully selected for the kind of upsets an organization wishes to generate. The executive team must identify the core competencies they wish to build, the soft spots in existing capabilities, and the projects that, if undertaken, will build new muscles.

Nordstrom's practice of providing extraordinary customer service necessarily places a great deal of stress on the system. But revealing the weak spots in a store's ability to respond to customer requests is the first step in strengthening those areas.

Others in Europcar's industry insisted that the company could not achieve its goal in less than two years; it would more likely take three. But Europcar, along with its partner in the project, Perot Systems, decided on an "impossible" 18-month deadline. Managers knew the resulting stress would reveal that Europcar's network of fiercely independent fiefdoms was preventing the company from competing successfully in the Pan-European market. Many country managers claimed that they did not have enough information on what was being designed and could never implement the new approach in time. Many also insisted on high degrees of tailoring to their individual country markets that ultimately would have compromised the new system's efficiency. These deep-seated territorial behaviors had to be exposed and surmounted if a true reinvention were to take place.

The purpose of generating breakdowns is to provide opportunities to enable both the organization and its executives to operate from the new context. Paradoxically, you can fail at the project (as has often happened on the road to scientific discoveries and in the careers of entrepreneurs) and still achieve a shift in being. Winston Churchill claimed that his repeated failures, from the disastrous Gallipoli invasion to defeat in his campaign for a seat in Parliament in the years between World War I and World War II, caused a sufficient shift in who he was to prepare him for the responsibilities of a wartime prime minister.

THOSE WHO CLIMB on the reinvention roller coaster are in for a challenging ride. The organization encounters peaks and troughs in morale, as initial euphoria is dampened by conflict and dogged task-force work. Morale rises again as alignment among stakeholders occurs—then recedes in the long and demanding task of enrolling the cynical ranks below. Reinvention is a demanding up and down journey—an adventure, to be sure. And it is destined to be that way.

Notes

1. We are indebted to numerous philosophers, scholars, and thinkers who have inquired into the nature of being, especially Werner Erhard, "Transformation and Its Implications for Systems-Oriented Research," unpublished lecture, Massachusetts Institute of Technology, Cambridge, Massachusetts, April 1977, and "The Nature of Transformation," unpublished lecture, Oxford University Union Society, Oxford, England, September 1981; Martin Heidegger, *What Is Called Thinking?* (New York: Harper & Row, 1968), *On the Way to Language* (New York: Harper & Row, 1971), *On Time and Being* (New York: Harper & Row, 1972); and Ludwig Wittgenstein, *Culture and Value* (Oxford: Basil Blackwell, 1980).

2. See Thomas P. Rohlen, "The Promise of Adulthood in Japanese Spiritualism," *Daedalus, Journal of the American Academy of Arts and Sciences,* Spring 1976, p. 125.

3. Numerous writers have grappled with the relationship of past, present, and future in the workplace, especially Werner Erhard, "Organizational Vision and Vitality: Forward from the Future," unpublished lecture, Academy of Management, San Francisco, California, August 1990; Edward Lindaman and Ronald Lippitt, *Choosing the Future You Prefer* (Washington, D.C.: Development Publi-

cations, 1979); Fritz Roethlisberger, *Training for Human Relations* (Boston: Harvard University, Graduate School of Business Administration, Division of Research, 1954); Marvin R. Weisbord, *Productive Workplaces: Organizing and Managing for Dignity, Meaning, and Community* (San Francisco: Jossey-Bass, 1991), pp. 282–85.

4. See Ikujiro Nonaka, "The Knowledge-Creating Company," *Harvard Business Review,* November–December 1991, pp. 96–97.

Originally published in November–December 1993
Reprint 93603

Changing the Mind
of the Corporation

ROGER MARTIN

Executive Summary

THE EXASPERATING THING about big companies in crisis is that they get there by doing the very things that once made them big. Roger Martin has been in the business of strategy consulting for 13 years and has only begun to appreciate how mechanically organizations resist new truths and how emotional this resistance can become.

The experience of troubled companies is a syndrome with four stages. First the founders articulate their vision. Then the company develops steering mechanisms to operationalize the vision and guide the company through change. Unfortunately, these steering mechanisms tend to become rigid over time, with much stronger ties to the founding vision than to the changing economic environment. So in the third stage, feedback deteriorates. And the useful signals that do get through run into organizational defensive routines—the fourth stage—that prevent information from being put to proper use.

The key to getting out of this syndrome—the key to achieving change—is to abandon blame and focus instead on what the company did *right* to get into the crisis it now faces. To answer that question, managers must examine the differences between the strategy the company *espouses*—the founder's vision, the steering mechanisms—and the strategy it *enacts*—the company's actual behavior with customers and competitors. The problem is not that one or the other of these two strategies is necessarily wrong, but that all too often they conflict.

The author talks about this conflict in his own firm and in client companies and offers suggestions for its resolution by means of reverse engineering, data testing, strategic dialogue, scientific discipline, and the development of new measures of progress.

THE MOST EXASPERATING FACT about big companies in crisis is that they got there by doing what once made them big. They come by their troubles honestly. This irony may seem manageable to people hoping to turn things around; but I have been in the business of strategy consulting for 13 years, and I am only now beginning to appreciate how mechanically organizations resist newer truth—and how strong the emotions are that underlie these mechanisms. Perhaps I should begin with a story.

One of my first clients was the CEO of a packaged foods company with whom I supposed I had been working extremely well, analyzing data on customers, competitors, and new technologies—the technical evidence. About a year into our relationship, the company was given the opportunity to acquire a snack business, which I was sure it should pass up. I proved with bulletproof logic that the company in question was the third competitor in a market where only two could survive. There was room for one brand leader and one low-cost producer; there was no point in being the challenger in either category.

For many months, the CEO and I reviewed this bit of strategic reasoning, and I was certain that my client understood the point. Yet a few months later, I discovered that he bought the snack business anyway, as soon as the price dropped "to an incredibly good number."

Obviously, something other than pure strategic reasoning had been poised to assert itself all along—something powerful but unacknowledged beneath the surface of our conversation, something my client was inevitably going to fall back on as soon as the right conditions presented themselves. In fact, this something was the assumption, second nature to the whole of top management since virtually the company's inception, that a consumer packaged foods company with brand recognition, good advertising, and acceptable market share was bound to make money, *deserved* to make money. Besides, the unarticulated argument continued, any company can be turned around with a little elbow grease, especially if you buy it cheap enough.

And then again, maybe not. In practice, the company has lost money on the snack business every year since acquiring it. But the case stands out in my mind not for what the client learned but for what I learned. As a consultant, my product was supposed to be strategic action, not just strategic brilliance. If my client failed to get the message, then I hadn't done my job. In fact, this is the story of a consultant, locked in his own inertial assumptions, becoming as blind to the needs of the client as the client was to the dynamics of the market. I had not yet come to realize that to catalyze change, I would have to see beyond cognitive instruction, beyond studies and presentations, to a process of learning more subtle and compassionate than anything I and most of my colleagues in the profession have practiced up to now. All change managers need lessons of this kind.

The key to the process is self-examination. Chris Argyris has written about how individuals in companies, even highly educated professionals, engage in what he calls organizational defensive routines to preserve their status and abiding sense of security (see "Teaching Smart People How to Learn," *Harvard Business Review,* May–June 1991). In searching for the source of any problem, they always look outside themselves and often outside the company, blaming the stupidity of the customer or client, the vagueness of strategic goals, or the unpredictability of the environment. In my view, however, organizations defend against change not because they are just like insecure individuals, but because they are made up of individuals (many of whom are, indeed, insecure) who are working at what always has worked. So what change managers first need to understand is the peculiar ways their company's practices provide an unfolding context for inertia.

Companies don't make the most of new opportunities because they're making the most of old ones.

Now, some will say the great challenge for change managers is to get employees to understand customers, not their own company. But it turns out that they can't understand customers unless they've understood themselves, and this means, first of all, understanding something like their company's life story.

If a company can be said to have a "mind," managers cannot change it merely by frightening themselves with reports of quarterly losses. Rather—like individuals—the collective leadership of companies needs first to look back, to find out the *good* reasons why they have come to act the way they do. They get control of their future by examining their past. They change by looking in, not out.

The Tragic Life of Troubled Companies

The experience of troubled companies is a syndrome with four discernible stages. There may be more, but I have found these enough to stimulate the right kind of debate among senior managers. First is the articulation of a *founder's vision*; second, the consolidation of *steering mechanisms*; third, the deterioration of necessary *feedback*; and, fourth, the proliferation of *organizational defensive routines*. By the last stage, corporations have created a world in which managers not only cannot see what is salient in their markets, they have gradually become impervious to learning of every kind.

THE FOUNDER'S VISION

Every company begins with a vision, comprised of two wedded elements: a product concept aimed at a particular market and a notion of the way the company needs to be organized to make the most of the market opportunity. Henry Ford did not simply develop a standard car for a mass market, he developed a system of mass production in which, not coincidentally, his own workers might afford the very cars they built. Similarly, Bill Gates's Microsoft not only designs software for personal computers, the company is its own best evidence that individuals networked by personal computers can be organized into value-adding teams.

Ford Motors and Microsoft are, of course, extraordinary examples of the ways the market vision and the corporate organization may develop reciprocally, which is why they have become signature companies of their respective times. But all big companies once originated a vision of competitiveness that was more or less valid for their market and industry.

Implicitly or explicitly, the founders correctly assessed customer needs, barriers, and rivals—and went for broke. They married their original assets to activities and processes that got them customers and cash. Then they reinvested, developing new assets—financial, physical, human, and scientific—trying to pattern these in ways that were new but still served their original vision. The Model A did not have to be black like the Model T, and, eventually, Henry Ford learned to live with the UAW. More recently, the MS-DOS handbook has been superseded by graphical interfaces.

In short, companies survive by growing in virtuous ways: growing into what once seemed pristine competitive space; growing a complex mix of financial, material, and knowledge assets; growing their market scope; growing the practical routines that make winning with customers replicable and standard. The problem is that competitive spaces shift, customers change, new technologies appear, and, ironically, it is when responding to markets transformed by intense and unpredictable change that big businesses are most confounded by patterns of past success. IBM's mainframe data processors, its proprietary distribution channels, even its gray-flannel suits, seemed positively avant-garde back in the 1950s.

Crisis is the privilege of survival. Companies fail to make the most of new opportunities because they are still doing their best to make the most of old ones.

STEERING MECHANISMS

All of this raises the question of how the company operationalizes the founder's vision, that is, how managers put critical elements of the vision into practice and, in so doing, deliberately but also inadvertently structure the perceptions and acts of their employees. This structure consists of dozens of nearly imperceptible steering mechanisms with which the company learns to keep itself afloat and on course as it grows. Steering mechanisms are thus the processes, assumptions, rules, and behaviors that are woven into systematic choice at all levels of the organization and in every discipline: budgeting and resource allocation, hiring and training, codes of conduct, strategy development, product development, norms of authority and succession. Steering mechanisms proliferate with the growing complexity of the company's task and make sense of otherwise chaotic market evidence.

Steering mechanisms are usually conceived with just two purposes in mind: to keep the organization aligned with the founder's vision and to keep the vision aligned with the economic environment. Each is indispensable to the company's success. At the same time, the inherent tension between the two is serious. In my experience, most companies have many steering mechanisms controlling for internal alignment with the vision. Fewer, sadly, control for changes in markets. And it is precisely when top managers try to catch up with an escaping market that the inertial force of their mechanisms becomes gallingly apparent.

The senior managers of a global telecom company I've worked with all agree that a new global product for tourists should not encroach on an offering designed for business travelers. But trying to get the managers of consumer products to collaborate with the managers of corporate accounts without inciting a turf war—turf staked out with great pain back when the company was broken into strategic business units—is a different story altogether.

DISRUPTED FEEDBACK

The most dangerous thing about obsolete steering mechanisms is the way they degrade market signals and fill managers' ears with noise. When a product concept goes wrong, we see managers seeking answers to the wrong questions. They gather reams of data, and all of it is more or less worthless because it supports a product strategy that is more or less worthless. Digital Equipment Corporation, for example, gathered extensive information on what customers wanted from its proprietary word-processing software without realizing that the age of proprietary minicomputers was over.

Obsolete steering mechanisms turn market signals into useless noise.

But something even worse can happen. Rigid steering mechanisms can cause managers to ignore complaints and other forms of unwelcome feedback that might be extremely valuable if they were put to appropriate use.

Take the case of a law firm I know whose founder's vision was simply the practice of "great law." When I asked the senior partners what their clients valued most about the firm, they said, "Insight, quickness, a 'can-do' attitude, congeniality." "Service" came last. In fact, these responses were more or less on target for some of the firm's most prized clients—legally sophisticated executives, many of them former lawyers, who came to the firm with special problems and who constituted its original bread and butter. But when some newer clients began to demand such things as detailed billing and greater timeliness, the senior partners began to resent their demands and lack of appreciation, as if the clients were asking thoroughbreds to deliver the milk.

What the firm failed to grasp was that, since its founding, it had migrated into another market, a necessary and lucrative market made up of corporate counsels whose priorities were more pedestrian and procedural. The firm might well have treated these corporate counsels differently, putting them into a distinct business category of their own, one focused on service, detail, and cost-effectiveness. But the partners were stuck in a pattern of response appropriate to delivering genius, not hand-holding.

People in companies fall back on rigid steering mechanisms as a matter of course, because this is what steering mechanisms are for. They "hard-wire" the strategy. They guide action when the unexpected happens—when there is a downturn in demand, say, or a crisis in recruiting. In this sense, steering mechanisms disrupt good feedback precisely because they are what *provided* good feedback when the company's earlier strategy was on target. They obscure new evidence with reaches for the older truth.

In the best of worlds, steering mechanisms would report on changes in the market and force the company to respond, and corporate learning would be continuous. This is not our world. There has never been a corporation that reinvents itself *as a matter of course*, and it is an open and fascinating question whether there ever could be.

DEFENSIVE ROUTINES

But some, eventually many, signs of trouble do get through. There are losses, defections, product failures; the stock price goes south. And when senior managers focus afresh on the future shape of their business— when, that is, they call in people like me—the exercise can be as disappointing as it is heady. I remember how in my earlier years as a consultant, the CEO and I would call urgent meetings, research customer needs from the bottom up, outline new and more efficient organizational structures and human resource policies, then articulate all of these findings as principles of action in a comprehensive, voluminous strategic plan— only to find that these principles, if not openly assaulted, died by a thousand cuts, while the strategic plan, if not openly rejected, was more or less systematically ignored.

The word "systematically" is critical, because few strategic plans are the victims of bad faith or employee sluggishness. To use terms of art borrowed once again from Chris Argyris, it is rather that any newly *espoused* strategy, however explicit and sensible, inevitably comes up against an implicitly *enacted* strategy supported by all the aged, compounded steering mechanisms that the company already has in place.

Why is this? Because people are not at their best when faced with a largely uncertain future. Traumatized by past events, they determine never, never to make the same mistake again—and wind up mistaking the old crisis for the new one. They fear for their jobs or for the jobs of the people who have been counting on their judgment. They fear their bosses or their boards. They avert their eyes from quantitative evidence contradicting their expectations. They snap at people who give voice to their repressed doubts. They demonize the competition, scoff at customers, infantilize themselves, and parentalize the CEO.

In short, people in corporate crisis are in no frame of mind to learn new facts of life, which is just what they need to do. The two most common defensive reactions I have seen implicitly glorify the past, and with the past, current—failing—practice. First, managers act out of a deep fear of inadequacy with respect to the founder. They think, "Billion-dollar visions do not grow on trees; who are we to question the manifest demonstrations of the founder's competence?" The inference for action is self-accusation: "Let us redouble our efforts; the problem is in our execution."

This kind of thinking almost killed the Ford Motor Company after Henry Ford died; it clearly hampered Digital Equipment's ability to refocus on personal computers right up until Kenneth Olsen's retirement. Even in businesses that are generations removed from their founders, the reputations of past leaders can weigh on the shoulders of current management like alps. Think about the residual weight of Alfred Sloan's decentralized divisional structure at General Motors.

A second reaction, parallel with the first, is the tendency of managers to idealize sunk assets. They travel from a European mill to a South American mine and take pride in the scope and grandeur of their company's activities. But this pride, a positive thing in good times, can become a serious handicap when dramatic change is in the offing.

The top managers of an integrated apparel company I know have come to understand that they are increasingly in a logistics business and that they will have to be low-cost producers upstream no matter how prosperous the corporation's various downstream businesses may become. But this does not mean that managers of weaving mills will readily agree to shut down inefficient plants, not as long as they can shift costs to cut-make-and-trim plants through transfer pricing. This practice was taken for granted, even encouraged, back when the company had come to the conclusion that vertical integration was the source of premiums—and the wave of the future besides. Now it had become a crippling flaw.

Consulting companies are hardly immune to the troubled-company syndrome, though our defensiveness is usually couched, predictably, in misconceptions about the ways our *clients* change. When I began in this business in the early 1980s, strategy consultants all assumed that change was purely a technical problem—witness my approach to the packaged foods client. We thought we could teach managers their own competitive advantage. We thought companies in crisis had simply not yet understood their industry structure, or did not understand their competitor's position, and that clever analytical use of our more subtle models of competitive advantage would surely lead clients to a kind of epiphany.

When my colleagues and I started our own company, we advanced this idea a step or two. Because our clients often had trouble wrapping their minds around the radical and counterintuitive ideas we so often came up with, we determined that we would teach clients everything we knew—our strategic language, our methodologies, our frames of reference—in gradually deepening levels of nuance and detail. We worked in teams with our clients' employees; they would, we thought, internalize both the process and results of our deliberations.

This—our *own* founder's vision—worked well enough. We put ourselves on the map; we made good livings. But we still often engendered diagnosis without action, analysis without catharsis. I was often exasperated, like a revivalist preacher who prompts a chorus of "amens" during the evening but inspires precious little virtue the next morning. And, like those lawyers I had consulted to, we had developed our very own defensive routine, which was secretly to belittle clients for their lack of imagination. It took us some time to learn how to unpack our own embedded assumptions, to learn the difference between business ignorance and business tragedy.

Structuring the Debate

How should managers set about changing the company's mind? How does one get action? If there is a governing principle, it is that change managers need to be as curious and serious about the psychodynamics of their organizations as they are about their technical analyses. They need to cultivate a mature sense of how people learn and cope—not something freshly minted MBAs commonly have a talent for—at the same time as they begin to work on strategic analysis. And the task, by the way, is *both/and*, not *either/or*. A manager or consultant who starts employees talking about their feelings without any reference to the company's measurable activities will launch bull sessions—not strategic debate.

The key, in other words, is to structure the course of rigorous strategic debate in a way that takes into account the dignity and defenses of people facing hard choices. There is no one way to do this, but the most successful managers I've worked with begin by acknowledging the tragic

*The question is: What did we do **right** to get into the crisis we now face?*

pattern of corporate crisis that I've just mapped out. The CEO makes clear to everyone that the company is in crisis not because people have damaged it, but because good practices have outlasted their useful lives.

No blame—that's crucial. The question all managers should be encouraged to ask—and it *is* often helpful to have outsiders come in to help ask it—is what things did we do *right* in order to get into the crisis we now face? What was our founder's vision, and what mechanisms did we put in place to make it come to life, day after day, year after year? And what data do we need to see how much of that vision still works?

Recently, I've been working with a furniture maker whose genius has been to design high-quality, ergonomically correct office furniture that can nevertheless be mass-produced. For a generation, competition in this niche was negligible, and margins were handsome. No more. So the senior managers and I gathered for two days, simply to tell and retell the story of the company's successes. In retrospect, perhaps the most important piece of the exercise was giving each senior manager an opportunity to formulate some personal wisdom about the company's founding. In this atmosphere of positive reminiscence—vaguely like the atmosphere of mourning, and having many of the same virtues—defensiveness fell away.

What had gone wrong? No one was quite sure. Most expressed enormous pleasure in the company's designs. Many took satisfaction in the civility of the workplace. Still, what clearly emerged from everybody's version was that despite its espoused customer-oriented strategy, the company had never actually segmented its customers—senior managers literally didn't know who the customers were.

Ordinarily, this might have been cause for some embarrassment. But in the context of positive soul-searching, the fact that the company had never segmented its customers didn't seem so egregious. After all, they had been successful with an enacted strategy that one of my colleagues has called the Field of Dreams approach—"If you build it, they will come." Now that the time had come for the company to behave more deliberately, segmentation could be the first priority.

Reverse Engineering the Enacted Strategy

In the course of discovering how a company got into trouble, it is critical to find out what the company is really thinking. By this I do not mean finding out what managers believe the strategy to be, but rather what makes up the company's "unconscious"—the buried principles of strategy enacted in what managers routinely do with customers, suppliers, employees, and each other.

How do you do this? In effect, you reverse engineer the whole corporate "mind" by looking in detail at just what the company does—those steering mechanisms I

spoke about. I once worked with an auto parts supplier
that espoused a strategy of upgrading to meet the
quality program of the
automaker that was its
customer. The auto-
maker, in turn, espoused
a close, cooperative, long-
term partnership with its
suppliers. This partner-
ship was supposed to involve data sharing, long lead
times, exclusive contracts—all the certainties that allow
suppliers to be cost-effective, innovative, and reliable.

What managers **believe** *the strategy to be is less critical than the unconscious strategies played out in company behavior.*

Upon closer inspection, however, both my client and
its customer were engaging in so much wishful thinking.
The automaker, historically afraid of dependency on any
one supplier, routinely controlled the design and refused
to share much of anything about the design process.
Moreover, it dictated prices and pushed down suppliers'
margins about as far as they could go.

My client reacted by refusing to invest in innovation,
fearing every improvement would only create a premium
that the auto company would skim. It also refused to
share financial data, anticipating an even greater
squeeze on margins. Both companies played their hands
closer and closer to the vest, with predictable consequences. My client, in the words of a senior manager,
"got constantly jerked around—new specs, bad fore-
casts, no continuity." On its side, the automaker failed to
get the world-class suppliers it needed to be internation-
ally competitive.

The only way out of this impasse was to plot out the
enacted strategies of both companies and show them
how they were hostage to steering mechanisms fit for a
different form of competition—in this case, the world of

"price takers" that worked in the U.S. auto industry so long as the Big Three were a virtual monopoly. Managers at the automaker took a good look at the actual behavior of procurement officials, design engineers, and financial analysts. Supplier executives looked hard at the investments and quality improvements they were actually making. Once managers on both sides could put a name to what they were really doing, they could begin to stop. If they had continued to assume that their espoused strategies were real, they would simply have continued to irritate and undermine each other.

Or take the case of a large commercial baking company I worked with in Canada. The founder's vision had matured successfully, and the company plausibly considered itself the country's premier supplier of branded bread products. In theory, the company's strategy was to focus on consumers, whom it reached, in theory, with high-value-added, well-advertised products. However, when we began to look together at the strategy the company was actually enacting, we could clearly see that the sales force was focused overwhelmingly on the supermarket private-label trade. And retailers dictated the proportion of private-label to brand-name bread, the breadth of the product line, and relative pricing. The company, meanwhile, had dramatically cut back on its consumer advertising.

Cynicism and dysfunction both begin when managers start saying one thing and thinking another.

Through its steering mechanisms, the company was acting out the role of commodity producer for the trade. Its stated strategy, by encouraging an air of congenial unreality, was now only a barrier to seeing what the company had actually become. Václav Havel once wrote that corruption begins when people start saying one thing and thinking another. So does cynicism—and the management dysfunctions that inevitably flow from it.

At the baking company, middle managers heard their CEO speak of winning by building the business on "unique new product introductions supported by high levels of advertising." They then saw salespeople caving in to supermarkets and the chief financial officer telling the board that margins were too thin to sustain the current advertising budget. They quite naturally concluded that their leaders simply did not mean what they said— and that they had better be equally sly if they were going to survive.

Cynicism is a fate that seems to lie in wait especially for companies like this bakery, producers of well-known branded products whose managers have grown complacent in the prestige that universal recognition of the brand confers on them, like aging prima donnas too comfortable in their fame. Managers in such companies are quick to claim the prestige of their brand yet fear saying anything "demoralizing." Their skittishness produces relations that always *look* supportive. Even in critical meetings, people never vehemently disagree; everyone tries to "build on the comment" of the person just before. What generally follows these meetings is intense behind-the-scenes politicking and cutthroat memo writing.

A Dialogue of Science

Common sense tells us that a CEO has a simple choice once the enacted strategy has been surfaced: either explicitly go ahead with what the steering mechanisms are causing the company to do anyway, or endeavor to change course. And that is precisely the choice. I work with clients to explore the logic that underlies their enacted strategies, and in a way this exploration makes it possible for the company's leaders to test their convictions about what the company should do.

This usually means, first and foremost, analysis of customers. Think of that furniture company that had never done a simple market segmentation. Once the enacted strategy came into relief, it was obvious that fundamental market research was warranted—indeed, people were suddenly eager for it. That apparel company, too, began to look with renewed interest at the demand for cloth, the shifts in cotton prices, the long-term prospects of fabric suppliers getting out or coming in. In both companies, managers became curious about quantitative market data of all kinds, because they now knew just what hypotheses needed to be validated or disproved.

Another way of saying this is that the collective exercise of teasing out the enacted strategy unleashes senior managers' scientific imagination. The question "What do we do now?" does not. Indeed, looking at enacted strategy should be encouraged in the whole of management—ultimately, the whole of the company. I don't mean publishing decisions that have already been taken—say, announcing in the company newsletter the purchase of a mill. On the contrary, CEOs who think that they get change by the force of command or that they preserve prestige by preserving secrets are mired in the status quo.

People are naturally scientific. They must see the reasons for change.

To get change in a great old company, thousands of grown men and women whose children depend on their acting prudently must see the rationale for change and view it with favor. They must see the reasoning behind a new strategic direction and understand the methods used to shape the supporting data—so that everybody can make or imagine themselves making the calculations for themselves. Besides, people are naturally scientific: they make hypotheses, collect information, criticize each other's demonstrated conclusions. The challenge is to channel this energy into an open discourse on the fate of the company, not into an underground discourse on the prejudices of the CEO.

There are, of course, many ways to generate and develop strategic dialogue of this kind: meetings, off-site gatherings, quality circles. The most exciting way my colleagues and I have found is computer-generated, competitive simulations—war games, as it were—in which managers model the competitive battlefield and practice a kind of company doctrine with one another. (The plummeting costs of computer processing power and software is making this more and more feasible, even for midsize companies.)

To compete, companies must burn themselves down every few years and rebuild their strategies, roles, and practices.

Of course any strategic dialogue has to focus on what we might call the strategic curriculum—methodologies, language, the ways data will be researched and captured in the future—and needs to include a discussion of how to conduct the discussion itself—organizational boundaries, role definitions, decision processes, codes of conduct, reward systems. Companies have to get used to the fact that the new competition will force them to "burn themselves down" and rebuild every few years. Setting the terms of a continuing strategic conversation will help make people more willing to expose their implicit models (of products, markets, customers) for testing and inquiry.

Can this strategic dialogue be permanent? Can a company introduce steering mechanisms that keep all other steering mechanisms open for reevaluation? Perhaps this is a convoluted way of asking whether or not so-called learning organizations are really possible. My answer is that they are. They *must* be, given the new competition. But even if they are not possible, managers need to act as if they were.

At that telecom company we've worked with, where globalization is the new and somewhat daunting imperative, we interviewed dozens of managers and surfaced all manner of undiscussable problems. We asked managers what contradictions they saw between the globalization strategy and protecting the turf of their business units, what political problems they saw getting in the way of serving customers. Then we brought the answers, many of them extremely vexed, to senior managers and insisted on public debate. We also insisted on more public recognition for product teams that negotiated alliances with each other. We developed an analytical model to reckon the real demand for various products so that the profitability of various cross-team configurations could be debated with hard data and not as political footballs.

If "learning organizations" are not possible, we must still act as if they were.

And then we did something more. We asked what kinds of training programs, knowledge-capturing systems, and management styles the company would need to put in place if the strategic dialogue were to become a more or less routine part of doing business. We asked how the knowledge assets of the company could be continuously improved. We urged the company to settle on new strategic models, outlined the data it would need to animate the models, and proposed the terms of an ongoing dialogue. It is not yet clear whether or not this initiative will succeed. It is clear that management is betting the company on it.

New Methods, New Terms of Art

Just *how* companies come to decide about their strategic opportunities is, of course, another matter. Suffice it to say that companies have to look at buyers, suppliers, points of differentiation, relative cost position, the threat of new entrants, the determinants of substitutability, the intensity of rivalry—all the considerations Michael Porter has urged on us in his justly famous "five forces" analysis. It is important to keep in mind, however, that to uncover a discrepancy between enacted and espoused strategy is not necessarily to abandon one for the other. Rather, it is the occasion for determining real competitive advantage—and for developing the means to pursue it.

Take that law firm I mentioned earlier. There was a case where the enacted strategy the firm had inadvertently adopted—that of serving two very different client groups—was actually the right course for it. What the firm then had to do was develop a number of new practices to cope with corporate counsels who wanted better service.

The bread company, on the other hand, was squandering its brand—hence, its capacity for differentiation—by becoming a commodity supplier to the trade.

But it could not go back to being a prima donna either. Rather, it had to go forward in a new strategic direction and become a low-cost differentiator—excellent at flexible manufacturing and logistics but aggressive in pursuit of niche markets.

As for the auto parts company, there was nothing wrong with its espoused strategy. The problem was that the company and its main customer were caught in a cycle of mutual suspicion: both talked the talk, neither walked the walk.

But let us assume for the sake of argument that the full complement of a company's managers can come to agreement on whether to keep or abandon the enacted strategy and even on what new market opportunities require. The next step is to develop metrics that express how well the company is advancing toward its new strategic goals.

At this moment, something subtle and exciting happens. In using the metrics that tell how they are doing, managers suddenly begin to *become* the new company— their terms of discussion, their terms of art, propel them into choices and realities that are not yet quite born. That integrated apparel company I spoke about had suffered eight quarters of losses before its CEO and president told senior managers to unpack *its* founder's vision—that of a company whose mills and factories in government-dominated, low-wage countries had given it a reliable price advantage in distribution channels.

Once top management determined that the company would have to attend to shareholder value, a whole new strategic language began to emerge. Accordingly, managers all began to speak about pieces of the company— mills, logistics, consumer businesses—in a new financial vernacular. Were mills "value enhancing" or "value diluting"? Did the net present value of the downstream factories justify swapping them for lower cost upstream assets? The company began to become a leaner logistics business in the way managers began to buy into a new language of explanation, a new way of shaping data.

Or think of Motorola's Six Sigma program—a near archetype of managing change by changing the language around the strategy. At Motorola, every employee was brought into the loop. Even the bakers in the company cafeteria produced a quantitative measure for Six Sigma muffins. This is not as fanatical as it sounds. The fact is, companies do not change until a new strategic language finds its way to every corner. There are too many steering mechanisms in any company for the CEO to pilot everything from the bridge.

Getting Courage

Let me see if I can summarize the lesson: acknowledge the tragic pattern of corporate crisis; reverse engineer the steering mechanisms; subject the assumptions of the enacted strategy, espe-

You cannot change an organization without courage, and you cannot induce courage from above, not even by example.

cially market data, to measurable tests; open a strategic dialogue within the company; aspire to the freedom and discipline of scientists; redefine competitive advantage; develop measures to plot progress toward victory and a new strategic language to describe it.

That leaves one final point.

You cannot change an organization without courage, and you cannot induce courage from above, not even by example. What you *can* do, though, is make goals and methods transparent enough that your employees will be willing to take some calculated risks. You want hundreds of people making informed choices and taking timely action. You do not want them all second-guessing each other or wondering if the boss really means what he or she says.

Think again of that auto company procurement manager. Imagine that she awarded, say, a balance-shaft contract to a single supplier and then the supplier failed to deliver, shutting down the whole engine line in the process. In a company that had seriously enacted a strategy of manufacturing reform—just-in-time and total quality—in which everybody understood the point of the strategy and had access to the data on which it was based, the decision to rely on that supplier, however dismaying, would appear a noble failure. In a company that had *not* gone through the process of clarifying its strategy, the decision would seem to be sheer recklessness.

Of course, it would be greater recklessness for the company to stick to a world of price taking and supplier gouging. But it is too much to ask of any one employee to make the case for a whole strategy while trying to save her own neck. To have risked a single-source contract in the first place, she needs confidence that her colleagues understand her intentions—that there are widely shared and understood measures by which she can either justify her decision or learn something from her mistake.

In his essay "Shooting an Elephant," George Orwell confesses that, like other imperial policemen in Burma, he acted mostly against his will, mostly out of the desire not to "appear like a fool." People in companies act out of much the same impulses. The world inevitably changes; existing practices and principles of action inevitably become unreasonable. The point is, employees do not look foolish sticking to them. Only the company does.

Originally published in November–December 1993
Reprint 93607

Why Do Employees Resist Change?

PAUL STREBEL

Executive Summary

DESPITE THE BEST EFFORTS OF SENIOR EXECUTIVES, major change initiatives often fail. Those failures have at least one common root: Executives and employees see change differently. For senior managers, change means opportunity—both for the business and for themselves. But for many employees, change is seen as disruptive and intrusive.

To close this gap, says Paul Strebel, managers must reconsider their employees' "personal compacts"—the mutual obligations and commitments that exist between employees and the company. Personal compacts in all companies have three dimensions: formal, psychological, and social. Employees determine their responsibilities, their level of commitment to their work, and the company's values by asking questions along these dimensions. How a company answers them is the key to successful change.

Two case studies demonstrate the effectiveness of revising personal compacts. In the first, Strebel describes how the CEO of Philips Electronics, Jan Timmer, pulled the company back from the brink of bankruptcy by replacing a risk-averse culture with one in which employees were committed fully to the company's goals.

In the second, the author examines how Haruo Naito, the CEO of Eisai, a Japanese pharmaceutical company, anticipated potential crises and created the context for long-term change. Eisai's employees took the lead in revising their own personal compacts; as a result, the company accomplished a major strategic change. The message is clear. Whether facing an immediate crisis or pursuing a new long-term vision, leaders can overcome their employees' resistance to change by redefining their personal compacts.

CHANGE MANAGEMENT ISN'T WORKING as it should. In a telling statistic, leading practitioners of radical corporate reengineering report that success rates in *Fortune* 1,000 companies are well below 50%; some say they are as low as 20%. The scenario is all too familiar. Company leaders talk about total quality management, downsizing, or customer value. Determined managers follow up with plans for process improvements in customer service, manufacturing, and supply chain management, and for new organizations to fit the new processes. From subordinates, management looks for enthusiasm, acceptance, and commitment. But it gets something less. Communication breaks down, implementation plans miss their mark, and results fall short. This happens often enough that we have to ask why, and how we can avoid these failures.

In the Change Program at IMD, in which executives tackle actual change problems from their own companies, I have worked with more than 200 managers from 32 countries, all of whom are struggling to respond to the shocks of rapidly evolving markets and technology. Although each company's particular circumstances account for some of the problems, the widespread difficulties have at least one common root: Managers and employees view change differently. Both groups know that vision and leadership drive successful change, but far too few leaders recognize the ways in which individuals commit to change to bring it about. Top-level managers see change as an opportunity to strengthen the business by aligning operations with strategy, to take on new professional challenges and risks, and to advance their careers. For many employees, however, including middle managers, change is neither sought after nor welcomed. It is disruptive and intrusive. It upsets the balance.

Senior managers consistently misjudge the effect of this gap on their relationships with subordinates and on the effort required to win acceptance of change. To close the gap, managers at all levels must learn to see things differently. They must put themselves in their employees' shoes to understand how change looks from that perspective and to examine the terms of the "personal compacts" between employees and the company.

What Is a Personal Compact?

Employees and organizations have reciprocal obligations and mutual commitments, both stated and implied, that define their relationship. Those agreements are what I call personal compacts, and corporate change initiatives, whether proactive or reactive, alter their terms. Unless managers define new terms and persuade employees to accept them, it is unrealistic for managers to expect employees fully to buy into changes that alter the status quo. As results all too often prove, disaffected employees will undermine their managers' credibility and well-designed plans. However, I have observed initiatives in which personal compacts were successfully revised to support major change—although the revision process was not necessarily explicit or deliberate. Moreover, I have identified three major dimensions shared by compacts in all companies. These common dimensions are *formal, psychological*, and *social*.

The *formal* dimension of a personal compact is the most familiar aspect of the relationship between employees and their employers. For an employee, it captures the basic tasks and performance requirements for a job as defined by company documents such as job descriptions, employment contracts, and performance agreements. Business or budget plans lay out expectations of financial performance. In return for the commitment to perform, managers convey the authority and resources each individual needs to do his or her job. What isn't explicitly committed to in writing is usually agreed to orally. From an employee's point of view, personal commitment to the organization comes from understanding the answers to the following series of questions:

- What am I supposed to do for the organization?

- What help will I get to do the job?

- How and when will my performance be evaluated, and what form will the feedback take?

- What will I be paid, and how will pay relate to my performance evaluation?

Companies may differ in their approach to answering those questions, but most have policies and procedures that provide direction and guidelines to managers and employees. Nevertheless, a clear, accurate formal compact does not ensure that employees will be satisfied with their jobs or that they will make the personal commitment managers expect. Unfortunately, many managers stop here when anticipating how change will affect employees. In fact, performance along this dimension is tightly linked to the other two.

The *psychological* dimension of a personal compact addresses aspects of the employment relationship that are mainly implicit. It incorporates the elements of mutual expectation and reciprocal commitment that arise from feelings like trust and dependence between employee and employer. Though often unwritten, the psychological dimension underpins an employee's personal commitment to individual and company objectives. Managers expect employees to be loyal and willing to do whatever it takes to get the job done, and they routinely make observations and assumptions about the kind of commitment their employees display. The terms of a job description rarely capture the importance of commitment, but employees' behavior reflects their awareness of it. Employees determine their commitment to the organization along the psychological dimension of their personal compact by asking:

- How hard will I really have to work?

- What recognition, financial reward, or other personal satisfaction will I get for my efforts?

- Are the rewards worth it?

Individuals formulate responses to those questions in large part by evaluating their relationship with their boss. Their loyalty and commitment is closely connected to their belief in their manager's willingness to recognize a job well done, and not just with more money. In the context of a major change program, a manager's sensitivity to this dimension of his or her relationship with subordinates is crucial to gaining commitment to new goals and performance standards.

Employees gauge an organization's culture through the *social* dimension of their personal compacts. They note what the company says about its values in its mission statement and observe the interplay between company practices and management's attitude toward them. Perceptions about the company's main goals are tested when employees evaluate the balance between financial and nonfinancial objectives, and when they determine whether management practices what it preaches. They translate those perceptions about values into beliefs about how the company really works—about the unspoken rules that apply to career development, promotions, decision making, conflict resolution, resource allocation, risk sharing, and layoffs. Along the social dimension, an employee tries to answer these specific questions:

- Are my values similar to those of others in the organization?

- What are the real rules that determine who gets what in this company?

Alignment between a company's statements and management's behavior is the key to creating a context that evokes employee commitment along the social dimension. It is often the dimension of a personal compact that is undermined most in a change initiative when conflicts arise and communication breaks down. Moreover, it is the dimension along which management's credibility, once lost, is most difficult to recover.

Unrevised Personal Compacts Block Change

Looking through the lens of unrevised personal compacts, employees often misunderstand or, worse, ignore the implications of change for their individual commitments. At Philips Electronics, based in the Netherlands, employees' failure to understand changing circumstances drove the organization to the brink of bankruptcy.

In the early 1980s, Philips's reputation for engineering excellence and financial strength was unparalleled, and it was a prestigious company to work for. The company—which pioneered the development of the audio cassette, the video recorder, and the compact disc—recruited the best electrical engineers in the Netherlands.

Employees often misunderstand or, worse, ignore the implications of change for their individual commitments to the company.

Like many multidomestic European companies, Philips had a matrix structure in which strong country

managers ran the international sales and marketing sub-
sidiaries like fiefdoms. Local product divisions were
organized separately, and competition for resources
among the different business units was vigorous. Central
control was anathema, but the size and complexity of
headquarters in Eindhoven grew nevertheless. At the
same time, competition was intensifying. Despite its
continued excellence in engineering innovation, Philips
was having trouble getting new products to market in a
timely way. Margins were squeezed as manufacturing
costs slipped out of line in comparison with Sony's and
Panasonic's, and market share started falling even in the
company's northern European heartland, where Sony
was rapidly taking over the leading position. During the
1980s, two successive CEOs, Wisse Dekkers and Cor van
der Klugt, tried to redirect the company. Each, in his
time, hammered home the problems that needed cor-
recting: the pace and quality of product development,
slow time to market, and high manufacturing costs. The
two men communicated vigorously, reorganized, and set
up task forces on change. In Philips's 1989 annual
report, van der Klugt reported that he had redefined
management responsibilities to give product divisions
greater freedom to respond to competitive and market
pressures. Yet the projected improvements in costs and
market share did not materialize quickly enough. At the
end of van der Klugt's tenure, Philips was facing the
biggest operating loss in the company's history.

Why couldn't either of those seasoned professional
managers deal with the changes in the competitive environment? They understood the problems, articulated
the plans, and undertook the initiatives that we associate with change leadership. Yet each failed in his
attempt to redirect the company in time because

widespread employee support was missing. In fact, personal compacts in place at the time actually blocked change because there was little alignment between senior managers' statements and the practice and attitude of lower-level managers and their subordinates.

But the problem could have been predicted. During Philips's prosperous years, a tradition of lifelong employment was part of the company culture. Job security came in exchange for loyalty to the company and to individual managers. Informal rules and personal relationships dominated formal systems for performance evaluations and career advancement. Managers' job descriptions and position in the hierarchy set limits on their responsibilities, and operating outside those boundaries was discouraged. Subordinates weren't encouraged any differently. People weren't trying to meet challenges facing the company or even looking for personal growth. Position and perceived power in the company network determined who got what. And because seniority so directly affected an employee's career growth and level of compensation, workers had no incentive to work harder than people just above them or to exceed their boss's minimum expectations for performance.

Moreover, even when costs were demonstrably out of line and operating margins were declining, Philips had no effective mechanism for holding managers accountable for failing to achieve financial targets. Budget-to-actual variances were attributed to events outside the control of unit managers. And because of the limitations of financial reporting systems and a culture that encouraged loyalty over performance, no one was able to challenge this mind-set effectively.

None of that changed under Dekkers or van der Klugt. Managers and subordinates were not forced to

understand how the changes essential to turning the
company around would require them to take a fundamentally different view of their obligations. Neither
Dekkers nor van der Klugt drove the process far enough
to alter employees' perceptions and bring about revised
personal compacts.

By the time Jan Timmer took over at Philips in May
1990, the company faced a crisis. Net operating income
in the first quarter of 1990 was 6 million guilders compared with 223 million guilders the previous year, and
the net operating loss for the year was projected by analysts at 1.2 billion guilders. Timmer was an insider from
the consumer electronics division, where he had successfully stopped mounting operating losses. But the
scale of Timmer's challenge to turn the company around
was matched by the pressure on him to deal quickly and
effectively with the potentially crippling losses.

Orchestrating the Revision of Compacts

The revision of personal compacts occurs in three
phases. First, leaders draw attention to the need to
change and establish the context for revising compacts.
Second, they initiate a process in which employees are
able to revise and buy into new compact terms. Finally,
they lock in commitments with new formal and informal
rules. By approaching these phases systematically and
creating explicit links between employees' commitments
and the company's necessary change outcomes, managers dramatically improve the probability of hitting
demanding targets. To lead Philips out of its crisis, Jan
Timmer had to steer the company through those phases.

SHOCK TREATMENT AT PHILIPS

Although the competitive landscape around Philips had changed, the company and its employees had not. Employees' personal compacts favored maintaining the status quo, so resistance to change was imbedded in the culture. To achieve a turnaround, Timmer was going to have to reach deep into the organization and not only lead the initiative but also closely manage it. Getting people's attention was merely the first step. Persuading them to revise the terms of their personal compacts was a much bigger challenge.

Timmer's approach was a dramatic one; in fact, it was shock treatment. Shortly after becoming CEO in mid-1990, he invited the company's top 100 managers to an off-site retreat at Philips's training center in De Ruwenberg. There he explained the company's situation in stark terms: Its survival was in jeopardy. To reinforce the message, he handed out a hypothetical press release stating that Philips was bankrupt. It was up to the group in the room to bring the company back. Everyone would have to contribute. Operation Centurion had begun and, with it, the end of life in the company as all those in the room had known it.

From the start, Timmer's terms for change were tough and unambiguous, and those who didn't like them were encouraged to leave. In Operation Centurion, Timmer captured the mind-set he wanted and created the process he would use to focus managers' attention on the new goals. Extending the metaphor, Timmer offered his managers new personal contracts, which were like the assignments given officers by their superiors in the Roman army. In the ensuing Centurion Sessions, the terms of these new compacts would begin to take shape.

Drawing on benchmarking data on best-in-class productivity, Timmer called for an across-the-board 20% reduction in head count. He also stipulated that resources for essential new initiatives would have to come from within, despite deep cuts in expenses throughout the company. The meeting broke up to allow managers from each product division to come to grips with what they had been presented and to consider how they would respond. Before this initial session with Timmer ended, each of the division managers had orally agreed on targets for reductions in head count and operating costs. In subsequent discussions, those plans became formal budget agreements between Timmer and his Centurion managers: Each plan was signed by the presenting manager to signify his personal commitment to the terms. Performance would be measured against achievement of the targets and linked to individual bonuses and career opportunities. Personal commitments, binding agreements, and standards for performance would form the basis for the new personal compacts at Philips.

Personal commitments, binding agreements, and performance standards formed the basis for new compacts at Philips.

The De Ruwenberg meeting has become part of Philips's company lore. It underscored the urgency of the company's situation and set the stage for the compact-revision process that followed. In the days and weeks thereafter, Timmer maintained a high profile as he spread the message of Operation Centurion and the significance of the new personal compacts. Regular budget reviews gave him opportunities to reinforce his message about personal commitments to current goals. Ongoing meetings with Philips's top 100 managers were the forum for discussing long-term plans.

But Timmer knew that he could not accomplish his goals unless managers and subordinates throughout the company were also committed to change. Employees' concerns about this corporate initiative had to be addressed. Therefore, as the objectives for Operation Centurion came into focus at senior levels, plans to extend its reach emerged. Senior managers negotiated Centurion contracts with their business unit directors, and that group then took the initiative to the product-group and country-management teams. At workshops and training programs, employees at all levels talked about the consequences and objectives of change. Timmer reached out via company "town meetings" to answer questions and talk about the future. His approach made people feel included, and his direct style encouraged them to support him. It soon became clear that employees were listening and the company was changing. By the end of 1991, the workforce had been cut by 22%—68,000 people. Those who didn't meet the terms of their contracts were gone, including Timmer's successor in the consumer electronics division. Even at the top, the culture of patronage, social networking, and lifetime employment in exchange for loyalty became things of the past. When no one inside qualified, Timmer hired top managers from outside. As a result, by mid-1994, only 4 members of the original senior-management committee remained, and only 5 of the 14 were Dutch. A company survey in 1994 confirmed that employees had responded favorably to the changes and the new atmosphere: Morale and feelings of empowerment had soared. After fluctuating during the early nineties, Philips's financial performance recovered strongly in 1993 and 1994; operating income rose from (4.3%) of sales in 1990 to 6.2% in 1994 and the share price moved from 20.30 guilders to 51.40 guilders.

Of course, not every case is like Philips's. You do not need a crisis to revise personal compacts and get greater commitment. The contrasting example of Eisai, a Japanese health-care company, shows how far the understanding of personal compacts can take you when change is proactive.

CREATING THE CONTEXT FOR CHANGE AT EISAI

A small, family-owned company, Eisai was one of the original manufacturers of vitamin E, and it maintained a strong research commitment to natural pharmaceuticals. Over the years, it developed drugs for the treatment of cardiovascular, respiratory, and neurological diseases; by the end of the 1980s, such drugs comprised 60% of the company's sales. The company experienced steady, modest growth during that decade, and in 1989 sales reached 197 billion yen and profits approached 13 billion yen. But there were signs of potential trouble ahead. Eisai was spending a hefty 13% of sales on R&D—compared with an average of 8.5% in other companies—and between 1982 and 1991, only 12 of the company's 295 patent applications in Japan had been approved by regulatory authorities. Although it was the sixth-largest Japanese pharmaceutical company, Eisai was a relatively small player in an industry in which global competition was increasing while growth in the domestic market was slowing down.

In 1988, Haruo Naito took over as CEO and president from his father. Before that, he had chaired Eisai's five-year strategic planning committee. During that time, he had become convinced that the company's focus on the discovery and manufacture of pharmaceuticals was not sustainable for long-term growth against large, global competitors. In the absence of either a real or a perceived crisis, however, and in the face of deeply felt cultural traditions, changing direction at Eisai would require unusual leadership.

To accomplish strategic transformation, Eisai's CEO had to create a context for change.

In the tradition of Japanese family companies, Eisai had few formal rules of employment. Among the 4,000 employees, lifelong employment was the norm and career advancement and authority were based on seniority. Groups made decisions because failure by an individual would mean loss of face. And employees were not encouraged to step outside established roles to take on assignments beyond the scope and structure of the existing organization. Individuals were loyal both to their managers and to group norms, so they did not seek personal recognition or accomplishment. And because other Japanese companies operated in similar ways, there was no external competitive pressure to be different. To accomplish strategic transformation, Naito would have to create a compelling context for change and an inducement for employees to try something new—without disrupting the entire organization.

The employees themselves would have to take the lead in designing the formal terms of their personal compacts.

Several years after becoming CEO, Naito formulated a radical new vision for Eisai that he called Human

Health Care (HHC). It extended the company's focus
from manufacturing drug treatments for specific ill-
nesses to improving the overall quality of life, especially for elderly sick people. To accomplish that
mission, Eisai would have to develop a wide array of
new products and services. And that, in turn, would
require broad employee involvement and commitment.
Although Naito did not explicitly characterize Eisai
employees' commitments as personal compacts, he
clearly understood that individuals would have to accept new terms and performance standards that he
could not simply mandate. He had to encourage entrepreneurial and innovative activity and create an environment in which such efforts would be accepted
and rewarded. Indeed, for his vision of HHC to become
reality, Naito knew that employees themselves would
ultimately have to take the lead in designing the formal terms of their personal compacts.

In 1989, Naito announced his new strategic vision
and initiated a training program for 103 "innovation
managers" who were to become the agents for change
in the company. The training program consisted of
seminars on trends in health care and concepts of organizational change. It also gave employees a firsthand
look at patient-care practices by having them spend
several days in both traditional and nontraditional
health-care facilities where they performed actual nurs-
ing activities. At the end of the program, Naito
charged the innovation managers with turning the insights from their experiences into proposals for new
products and services. Each proposal was brought before Naito and Eisai's executive management to gain
high-level corporate support and, as important to
Naito, to secure individual managers' public commitment to the achievement of their HHC projects' goals.

This training program and the subsequent HHC product-development efforts set the stage for the creation of a dramatically different set of personal compacts at Eisai. The innovation managers operated outside both the normal organizational structure and the company's traditional cultural boundaries. They designed new products and programs, put together multidisciplinary teams to develop their ideas, and drew new participants of their own choice into the change initiative. They reported to Naito, and he personally evaluated their performance and the contribution of individual projects to the HHC vision. As a result, junior people had a chance to break out of the seniority system and to shape the development of the company's new strategy as well as the terms of their own personal compacts. These were opportunities previously unheard of in Eisai or in other Japanese pharmaceutical companies.

The visibility and senior-management support for the first projects generated widespread enthusiasm for participating in the new movement at Eisai. The cross-functional teams established employee ownership of the HHC vision, which rapidly took on a life of its own. Soon there were proposals for 130 additional HHC projects involving 900 people, and by the end of 1993, 73 projects were under way. New services offered by the company included a 24-hour telephone line to assist people taking Eisai medications. Another brought consumers and medical professionals together at conferences to discuss health care needs. New attention to consumer preferences led to improvements in the packaging and delivery of medications.

Although personal compacts at Eisai are still dominated by traditional cultural norms, Naito's ability to lead his employees through a process in which they examined and revised the old terms enabled them to accomplish major strategic change. The effects of the new strategy are visible in Eisai's product mix. By the end of 1993, the company had moved from sixth to fifth place in the Japanese domestic pharmaceutical industry, and today Eisai's customers and competitors view the company as a leader in health care.

Culture and Personal Compacts

The extent to which personal compacts are written or oral varies with the organization's culture and, in many cases, the company's home country. In general, the more homogeneous the culture, the more implicit the formal dimension of personal compacts is likely to be. The same is true along psychological and social dimensions in homogeneous environments, because employers and employees share similar perspectives and expectations. For example, in Japan and continental Europe, the legal systems for settling disputes are based on a civil code documented in statutes. Those systems carry over to the underlying principles in legal contracts and to the assumptions that support employer-employee relationships. Indeed, when a compact is laid out too explicitly in Japan, it is taken as an affront and a sign that one party doesn't understand how things work.

Personal compacts will need to be more explicit as companies become truly multinational.

By contrast, in countries like the United States, personal compacts tend to be supported by formal systems to ensure objectivity in the standards for performance evaluation. And more structure exists to support employee-employer relations, both in the form of company policies and procedures and in the role that human resource departments play. Similarly, as companies become more truly multinational, the importance of making the terms of personal compacts explicit increases, as does the requirement to support them formally. In my experience, this is true whether companies are implementing change to meet the needs of a culturally diverse workforce or to respond to market opportunities and threats.

Regardless of the cultural context, unless the revision of personal compacts is treated as integral to the change process, companies will not accomplish their goals. In one way or another, leaders must take charge of the process and address each dimension. Jan Timmer and Haruo Naito revised their employees' personal compacts using different approaches and for different reasons. But each drove successful corporate change by redefining his employees' commitment to new goals in terms that everyone could understand and act on. Without such leadership, employees will remain skeptical of the vision for change and distrustful of management, and management will likewise be frustrated and stymied by employees' resistance.

Originally published in May–June 1996
Reprint 96310

Reshaping an Industry

Lockheed Martin's Survival Story

NORMAN R. AUGUSTINE

It is not the strongest of the species that survives, nor the most intelligent; it is the one that is most adaptable to change.
—CHARLES DARWIN

Executive Summary

IN MOST INDUSTRIES, the loss of a few percentage points in the market is a severe setback, even a catastrophe. The U.S. defense industry has seen more than 50% of its market disappear, and the companies that make up the industry have faced the need for the equivalent of self-administered surgery with no insurance, no anesthetic, and no assurance of long-term health.

In 1995, Martin Marietta and Lockheed combined to form Lockheed Martin. That company has emerged in a most coveted role: survivor. In fact, it has seen its stock price nearly double in less than two years. In this article, CEO Norman Augustine relates the company's experience and offers some difficult—and painful—prescriptions.

For example, his first piece of advice: Read the tea leaves. The tremors of change in the defense industry began not when the Soviet Union imploded but when a new term entered the business lexicon: *financial engineering*. After narrow escapes from takeover attempts, both Martin Marietta and Lockheed learned that forced restructurings signal problems ahead.

Companies in turbulent industries need road maps—even when there don't seem to be any roads. And they must seize the opportunities for making large changes that upheaval provides. But companies such as Lockheed Martin can't afford to be distracted by change. It's easier said than done, but managers must stay focused on their business, their customers, and their most important asset: employees.

Companies in technology-driven industries must reinvent themselves continually. The bad news is that change requires hard decisions. The good news is that success awaits organizations willing to make those decisions.

THE U.S. DEFENSE INDUSTRY helped win the Cold War. Now it is engaged in another tremendous challenge: winning the peace. Every U.S. citizen has a stake in the future of the industry, which has played a vital role in modern life. It helped create the global village by inventing jetliner travel and space-based telecommunications, it spurred the development of digital computers, and it revolutionized access to space with the space shuttle and scientific probes to other planets.

Most industries consider the loss of a few percentage points in their market a severe setback, even a catastrophe. The companies that make up the defense industry have seen more than 50% of their market disappear—a disaster not widely understood by the public. Of course the world is relieved that nuclear holocaust is no longer considered a threat. But that very positive outcome tends to overshadow the everyday, real-world consequences that arise when an industry is forced to reengineer itself virtually overnight.

In the 1980s, most sectors of the industry went south. No sooner had the Berlin Wall tumbled than the U.S. government began chopping major portions out of the defense budget. Few would disagree that the post–Cold War United States could safely shrink its defense industry, and it surely has: defense procurement has declined by more than 60% in constant dollars since 1989. But what a time for the roof to leak—just when it started raining. Around the same time, NASA's budget and commercial airlines' spending on new planes simultaneously entered a power dive.

The severity of the impact on the defense industry has been devastating, exceeding that of the great stock market crash of 1929 on the U.S. economy as a whole, when about 29% of the nation's GNP eventually disappeared. Estimates suggest that only about one-quarter of the 120,000 companies that once supplied the Department of Defense still serve in that capacity; the others have shut down their defense lines of business or have dissolved altogether. And the surviving companies have laid off highly skilled, dedicated workers at the rate of one every 45 seconds for a number of years—a sustained rate of loss far greater than that experienced in any other industry in recent times.

In today's environment, defense companies seeking survival are faced with the need for self-administered

surgery with no insurance, no anesthetic, and no assurance of long-term health. While such high-profile
strategic alliances as the Lockheed-Martin Marietta-
Loral combination and the Boeing-McDonnell Douglas
and Raytheon-Hughes acquisitions have made the
front pages, the industry has been engaged in an even
more fundamental transformation. Those familiar with
the industry observe that the unlikely has become
commonplace and the unthinkable almost inevitable. A
satirical press release surfaced last year at the Pentagon asserting that Lockheed Martin's next acquisition would be the U.S. Air Force. When queried by a
senior Department of Defense official, I assured him
the press release was false: "We looked into the possibility, but your present owner has too much debt on
the books."

Despite the attempt at gallows humor, there is no
doubt that the U.S. defense industry, as well as many
other industries, live in Darwinian times. Survival
demands that companies combine with former competitors and mutate into new species. (See the exhibit
"Changing Contours in the U.S. Defense Industry.")
Lockheed Martin learned many lessons as it added battle scars to its battle ribbons. The most important lesson
became self-evident: there are only two kinds of companies—those that are changing and those that are going
out of business. As a European aerospace executive said
when describing the still inefficient operations of many
defense companies on the Continent, "There are many
of us dead now, we just don't know it yet."

In the midst of worldwide turbulence in the
aerospace market, the company I serve has emerged in
a most coveted role: survivor. For a brief moment, we
were referred to as a behemoth or an 800-pound

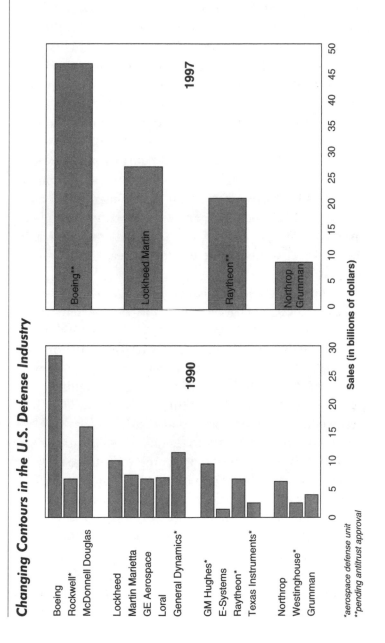

Changing Contours in the U.S. Defense Industry

Sales (in billions of dollars)

*aerospace defense unit
**pending antitrust approval

gorilla. With the proposed Boeing-McDonnell Douglas merger, we have assumed a more familiar standing: a very healthy David in a world of one Goliath. We can draw on our harrowing experience to set down some thoughts on how the process of transformation actually occurred and offer some prescriptions to others unfortunate enough to find themselves similarly challenged. It is all here: the startling nosedive of the marketplace and the equally dramatic rebound of Lockheed Martin. Despite the downturn in defense spending, we have seen our stock price nearly double in the less than two years that it has been listed on the New York Stock Exchange. In short, we have been growing while we shrank, leading many to wonder, in the words of a popular television series, How did they do that?

Perhaps the most critical moment in the defense industry's consolidation occurred in 1993, when then defense secretary Les Aspin invited a small number of CEOs of major defense companies to the Pentagon for dinner. After the meal, he and then deputy secretary William Perry served an unappetizing and highly prophetic fortune cookie: within five years, at least half of the companies represented at the dinner would not be needed to fulfill the nation's defense needs. Later, Perry even said, "We expect defense companies to go out of business, and we will stand by and let that happen." Much to the chagrin of most everyone present, I impertinently referred to the gathering as the Last Supper.

Following that meal, it became evident that there were only two potential survival strategies. One was to move into new markets—a difficult and time-consuming option that has rarely succeeded. The other entailed something almost as difficult: increasing market share in existing markets during a period of severely declining business.

We saw two ways to pursue either strategy. The first was external reengineering: combining companies through mergers or acquisitions. The second was internal reengineering: changing the way a company does business. Of course, those approaches are not mutually exclusive. All parties are best served when management delicately combines both. Is the process difficult? Restructuring a complex organization during a period of profound market decline is tantamount to rebuilding an aircraft while it is in flight—and loaded with passengers.

So far, we've succeeded. But it is hard to say exactly how. The writer W. Somerset Maugham observed, "There are three rules for writing a novel. Unfortunately, no one knows what they are." In lieu of two or three painless rules of restructuring yet to be discovered, I offer a dozen pretty good but sometimes painful rules that represent the best practices derived from the 17 companies that combined to form Lockheed Martin—as well as from our studies of several other prominent corporations that faced upheavals in their markets.

Regrettably, these rules are not based on elegant, esoteric theories; they are distilled from actual experiences. Adapting to a rapidly changing business environment is not fun, and managers most assuredly should not treat it like a spectator sport. There is a saying in the world of corporate finance that every time management tries something that works, economists invariably ask, "Would it have worked in theory?" In this case, I don't know if the rules work in theory—but they worked in practice.

I. Read the Tea Leaves

Financial wizard Warren Buffett once cautioned, "Beware of past performance 'proofs' in finance. If history books were the key to riches, the *Forbes* 400 would consist of librarians." After the defense industry's numerous successes over the years—from landing human beings on the Moon to helping defeat the fourth largest army in the world in just 40 days—we thought our grasp on the future was firm. We did not foresee that we were in the grip of something much greater: a world that was understandably eager to abandon its Cold War mind-set.

In all honesty, the tremors of change in the defense industry did not begin when the Soviet Union imploded. One could have read danger signs in the tea leaves in the early 1980s, when a new and ominous term entered the business lexicon: *financial engineering*. Both Martin Marietta and Lockheed were initiated early on. Martin Marietta was christened in 1982, the day the Bendix Corporation began a hostile takeover attempt. Having struck first, Bendix soon owned a majority of Martin Marietta's shares. Led by then CEO Tom Pownall, Martin Marietta retaliated by purchasing a majority of Bendix shares—a maneuver the media promptly dubbed the Pac-Man Defense after the little figures that gobbled up one another in the popular video game of the time. In retrospect, it is apparent that Martin Marietta was employing out-of-the-box thinking—not out of any attempt to be creative but

> *Don't wait until an industry is about to collapse to make crucial changes. Read the tea leaves early on and watch for danger signs.*

out of an urgent desire to survive. As a result, each company literally owned the other. By the time the predicament was finally settled, Martin Marietta found itself saddled with a debt-to-capital ratio of 82% as the corporation sought to buy itself back.

Our colleagues-to-be at Lockheed endured a similar trial by fire in 1989 and 1990, when the company found itself in play as a result of a proxy offer by a wealthy investor in Texas. Equally determined to maintain the company's independence, the board of directors—led by then chairman and CEO Dan Tellep—argued vigorously for stockholders' support. After two drawn-out proxy contests, Lockheed, too, managed to save itself.

The price of independence was high, but each company believed its actions were critically important for itself as well as for national security. Each company ended up with increased debt, and each further concentrated in the defense business—just in time for the collapse of U.S. defense spending.

The hard-and-fast lesson we learned is that forced restructurings, such as those that result from takeover attempts, usually signal problems ahead. The trick is to recognize the warning and act on it. To this end, all CEOs should have in a desk drawer a list of the worst things that could happen and a set of contingency plans. Three years ago, Martin Marietta made a friendly offer to purchase Grumman Corporation but was blocked by a higher bid from Northrop Corporation. We had anticipated the possibility of such a move, which is why we wrote a $50 million cancellation fee into our contract. Rather than get into a

Forced restructurings, such as those that result from hostile takeover attempts, usually signal problems ahead.

bidding war that could have ended with a Pyrrhic victory, we chose to take the $50 million and prepare for the other opportunities we were sure lay ahead.

II. Have a Road Map Even When There Are No Roads

As comedian Woody Allen said, "More than any other time in history, mankind faces a crossroads. One path leads to despair and utter hopelessness. The other, to total extinction. Let us pray we have the wisdom to choose correctly."

Choosing correctly is more easily said than done. Experts outside the defense industry usually propose that defense companies diversify into consumer-oriented businesses. Yet as far back as 30 years ago, the Arms Control and Disarmament Agency issued a report that found attempts at commercial diversification by U.S. defense companies "a discouraging history of failure." Six years ago, the ACDA revisited the matter and reported, "Successful examples of such conversion are difficult to find." And consider the observation of the president of a high-tech company in southern California that had lost one-half of its 100 workers in just a few years: "The person who thinks we can quickly beat our swords into plowshares has never tried it and probably never met a payroll." Defense conversion must be approached cautiously. The strategy can work, as indeed it has in some instances when companies have moved into adjacent commercial markets: markets that share technologies and customers with a company's established businesses. But conditions must be right, and expectations must be realistic.

Having read the tea leaves, both Martin Marietta and Lockheed chose to follow similar road maps in the early 1990s. Borrowing a strategy from the Japanese semiconductor industry, we each set out to increase market share in our core businesses—even during a period of economic downturn. We both also realized that consolidation with other companies would increase efficiency and competitiveness and would support expansion into adjacent commercial markets.

Lockheed and Martin Marietta each began to search for corporate partners. Neither company considered being the aggressor in a hostile transaction, for reasons bordering on the ethical—a sentiment that was heightened by each company's earlier escape from financial predators. Because both companies knew what it felt like to be the target of a takeover attempt, each resolved to treat any consolidation with another company as a combination of professional organizations instead of as a takeover or an acquisition. To signal that attitude, we use the word *combination* to describe our various alliances.

Lockheed soon purchased General Dynamics' aircraft business, and Martin Marietta purchased General

In truth, we are on a journey with no final destination and no resting points.

Electric's aerospace business, followed by General Dynamics' space business. Eleven months later, Lockheed and Martin Marietta joined in a merger of equals to form the Lockheed

Martin Corporation. Soon after, Lockheed Martin Corporation purchased Loral Corporation, resulting in today's Lockheed Martin. All told, our company comprises 17 previously independent entities: General Dynamics' tactical-aircraft and space-systems divisions, Sanders, Gould Ocean Systems, GE Aerospace, RCA Aerospace, Xerox Electro-Optical Systems, Goodyear Aerospace, Fairchild Weston, Honeywell Electro-Optics, Ford Aerospace, Librascope, IBM Federal Systems,

Unisys Defense, Lockheed, Martin Marietta, and Loral, including LTV Missiles.

Through this unprecedented series of combinations, Lockheed Martin emerged as the top provider to three key government customers: the Department of Defense, the Department of Energy, and NASA. We are the world's leader in building satellites and the U.S. leader in launching spacecraft. And despite our downsizing, we were ranked for the first time among the *Fortune* 25. Our road map indeed delivered us to our desired position, but, in truth, we are on a journey with no final destination and no resting points.

III. Move Expeditiously

An old English proverb states, While the doctors consult, the patient dies. Once a strategy has been established, moving expeditiously is critical to success. Why? Because mergers, acquisitions, and reengineerings have so many moving parts that if one part stalls, the entire endeavor may grind to a halt. Announce an ambitious schedule and keep to it. It is better to be 80% correct and make the change happen than to be 100% correct after the opportunity has passed. Most shareholders won't accept the excuse a professional football coach gave after his team lost a close game: "We didn't lose; we just ran out of time."

Consider the Martin Marietta-GE Aerospace combination in 1993, in which a total of only 27 days elapsed between the first meeting of the CEOs and the announcement of the fully documented contract. Unfortunately, the mandatory government-review process that followed took another four months. During the review, the two companies' stocks collectively increased in value by about $9 billion, presumably in anticipation of the deal's consummation. If a snag had developed during this review period, both companies' stocks most likely would have plummeted, with ominous implications for the companies' balance sheets, their customers' confidence, and their employees' morale—and for future consolidation in the industry. The danger is real: in 1992, nearly ten months passed before a federal judge finally denied Alliant Techsystems' proposal to buy Olin's ordnance division on the grounds that the acquisition would violate antitrust laws. Both companies suffered substantial losses.

As reflected in the Alliant-Olin case, antitrust laws or, more precisely, the process of *applying* antitrust laws, creates uncertainty. In our experience, the review process was competently administered and prudently executed, but not in a fashion one could ever call efficient. Each stage involved month after month of painstaking and time-consuming work to prepare carton upon carton of documentation, during which time the companies involved were essentially in a state of suspended animation. The U.S. government and other interested parties need to revise the review process as well as other government approval processes, such as those conducted by the Department of Defense, to reflect the fast-forward reality of the global marketplace in the twenty-first century.

IV. Make Megachanges

Upheaval provides a rare chance to initiate large changes throughout a business—changes that may make even greater restructuring down the road unnecessary. By far the most radical change I have observed in the aerospace industry was spearheaded by Kent Kresa,

who was CEO of the company formerly known as
Northrop. Kresa's approach was described in the May 17,
1990, issue of *USA Today*: "CEO Kent Kresa also said
Northrop will continue to sell non-productive assets.
Last year, it sold its headquarters in Los Angeles."

To achieve megachanges, it is important to set goals
that may seem unattainable, motivate people to reach
those goals, and give them the resources to do so. Jack
Welch set demanding goals at GE, and after a decade of
his leadership, the company is producing three times the
profit with three-quarters of the workforce. Similarly,
the companies that today make up Lockheed Martin
have closed about 16 million square feet of plant space—
about one-fourth of all our original plant space. Our collective workforce has been reduced by more than
100,000, leaving us with a workforce two-thirds the size
it might have been. Through restructuring *alone*, we
have produced recurring annual savings of about $2.6
billion—about 10% of our overall cost of doing business—not including the additional savings generated in
the ordinary course of operations.

Fundamental changes in management style save
money as well. As stated in *Augustine's Laws*, "If a sufficient number of management layers are superimposed
on top of each other, it can be assured that disaster is
not left to chance." Peter Drucker, the dean of American
management, wrote, "When, during the past 10 or 15
years, companies began to organize themselves internally around the flow of information . . . they immediately found that they did not need a good many management levels. Some companies have since cut two-thirds
of their management layers." Today these companies
grow increasingly efficient as they reduce management
layers to eight, six, or even fewer.

My experience, especially in organizations such as the Pentagon, has convinced me that having deputies is counterproductive except under the most extraordinary circumstances. Two heads may be better than one, but not if they're occupying the same box on an organization chart. Similarly, when combining two organizations, don't just let them fly in close formation. Insist that they be fully integrated and streamlined from the bottom up—*all* the way up.

In this effort, it is important to delegate most decision making to the lowest level at which a considered judgment can be made. That time-honored philosophy too often seems to be lost in the modern organization. Mort Feinberg, an industrial psychologist, harks back to biblical times when he tells how Jethro, father-in-law to Moses, observed that great confusion reigned as Moses led his people out of Egypt. Jethro remarked that Moses seemed to be sitting alone while everyone else stood waiting for direction. It has been said that Jethro's observation qualified him as the world's first management consultant—a somewhat dubious accomplishment in my book! He advised Moses, "What you are doing is not good. You and the people with you will wear yourselves out, for the thing is too heavy for you; you are not able to perform it alone."

V. To Think Outside the Box, Get Outside the Box

It's hard to be creative in the press of business. Too many demands keep us from exploring unfamiliar solutions. Consider the opening lines in A.A. Milne's classic, *Winnie-the-Pooh*, and try to avoid a similar fate: "Here is Edward Bear, coming downstairs now, bump, bump,

bump, on the back of his head, behind Christopher Robin. It is, as far as he knows, the only way of coming downstairs, but sometimes he feels that there really is another way, if only he could stop bumping for a moment and think of it."

In the 1980s, NASA challenged Lockheed Martin to cut the weight of the huge fuel tank that forms the structural backbone of the space shuttle by several thousand pounds. The effort stalled at the last 800 pounds. As the blue-ribbon engineering team turned its attention to increasingly exotic lightweight materials—which often seemed to be derivatives of "unobtainium"—one of the line workers made a suggestion: stop painting the tank. The 200 gallons of white paint that covered the tank added 800 pounds to a device whose life span in flight was only about eight minutes and whose fate was to end up at the bottom of the Indian Ocean. Sometimes the best way to think outside the box is to listen to someone who is outside the box.

The importance of thinking outside the box also applies at the level where corporate goals are developed. Strategically, we try to anticipate where our industry will be in 5, 10, and even 20 years. We believe in the wisdom once expressed by the hockey star Wayne Gretzky, who explained his success by saying, "I skate to where the puck is going to be, not where it has been." For example, today's military aircraft and fighting ships will have to last for decades, but the electronic and other technology-intensive parts may become obsolete in five years or less (software components are sometimes eclipsed in as little as one or two years). After decades of focusing on building airplanes, the industry is coming to realize that what you put on airplanes has to be replaced more frequently than the airplanes themselves. Succeeding in such a market requires us to get out of the box of being primarily airframe builders. Today electronic and other technological upgrades are becoming an ever greater focus of Lockheed Martin's lines of business. We realize that technology is a moving target, and we act accordingly.

The history of tactical aircraft since the days of the Wright brothers shows that the cost of each airplane has been increasing at an unvarying rate. By 2054, if that rate continues, the cost of a single combat airplane will equal the entire projected defense budget. Obviously, we can't stand by and let that happen. We have to find a way out of the dizzying upward spiral. To that end, Lockheed Martin has made major investments in innovative technologies to reduce costs. Those investments contributed considerably to our recent win of a Joint Strike Fighter contract, which could lead to billions of dollars of sales.

VI. Benefit by Benchmarking

It is essential to set goals, monitor progress, and provide feedback throughout any period of restructuring. It is also important to be able to quantify results in the end. One must strenuously avoid the fog in which an unfortunate Marine Corps official found himself when asked about the expected cost of a new helicopter. "The estimate is based on an estimate," he conceded.

Keeping score in business begins with establishing important indices, such as financial results and process measures, and then recording and sharing them with members of the workforce who can make use of that knowledge. We have found, for example, that cycle time is a very important measure of performance, as is the first-time-inspection acceptance rate. Other useful measures include scrap and rework, touch-labor content, and total yield, to name but a few. Of course, it is critical to focus on the right measures and always be alert to the danger of misinterpretation. As movie producer Sam Goldwyn is said to have replied when told the script he wanted to produce was too caustic, "'Too caustic?' To hell with the cost. If it's a good picture, we'll make it."

One high-profile example of benchmarking is exemplified in our space-shuttle-servicing program. Using a 15-year history of costs accumulated on the shuttle program, NASA and United Space Alliance, a joint venture of Lockheed Martin and Boeing, have entered into an innovative agreement to service the shuttle program that will maintain safety, meet flight schedules, and reduce costs by an estimated $400 million over the next six years. The contract reflects performance-based requirements and would be impossible to implement if United Space Alliance did not have hands-on experience setting and meeting such strict parameters.

It is also essential to ask customers how *they* think you match up against the measurements that are important to *them*. In many of Lockheed Martin's contracts, customers determine our fee based on their unilateral judgment of our performance. For 1996, the company's median fee, which can range from zero to 100% of the target, was 93%. In one-fifth of the cases, we received a 100% rating. Of course, one index is even more telling: do customers buy the product? The original business plan for Lockheed Martin's E-ZPass electronic toll-collection system, which is now used by New York's MTA Bridges and Tunnels, estimated sales of 170,000 electronic tags within three years. In fact, 280,000 cars had tags within *one* year.

Bringing out the natural competitive instincts in human beings is a powerful way to enhance efficiency while instilling a sense of pride and encouraging teamwork. This tactic can work wonders even when the competitor is oneself, as is so vividly evidenced by the durability of the game of golf. At Lockheed Martin, we grade the performance of each company, each sector, and the corporation as a whole at the end of each year. Needless to say, a great deal of comparing takes place year to year and among sister organizations.

VII. Don't Lose Sight of Day-to-Day Business

There are no footnotes to the stock listings that state, "Temporarily excused due to restructuring." No matter what is going on inside a company, there is still a company to run. Management cannot adopt the attitude exhibited by a local bus service in rural England, whose drivers passed by long queues of would-be passengers with a smile and a wave of the hand. "It is impossible for the drivers to keep their timetables if they must stop for passengers," explained one of the company's officials. The logic is certainly impeccable, but something seems to have been missed.

At Lockheed Martin, we can't afford to be distracted by organizational change. We have no margin for error. About 20 years ago, a U.S. spacecraft veered into outer space on a useless trajectory because one hyphen had been omitted from the tens of thousands of lines of software code that guided the craft. In another case, a major spacecraft proved to be badly nearsighted because of a minute grinding error in the optical train's primary mirror. And the failures caused by a tiny speck of dust are legion. Nothing focuses the attention like watching a friend climb into an experimental aircraft or on top of a rocket containing 500,000 gallons of liquid oxygen and liquid hydrogen. Spending a career trying to defy the law of gravity is a humbling endeavor. Mother Nature is a fair judge but an extremely unforgiving one.

Lockheed Martin is currently responsible for many of the nation's most advanced communications satellites orbiting Earth. Among these are a series of military satellites built by Lockheed. They contain components provided by GE and technology developed by RCA, and they were launched by Martin Marietta with ground support from Loral. The fact that acquisitions and mergers took place among all those companies is completely irrelevant to the customer—and, for that matter, to the laws of physics that often determine the success or failure of such projects.

It is difficult to overemphasize the complexity of meeting such challenges in an environment of continual change. Perhaps the most instructive example in Lockheed Martin's experience occurred as we were moving a half-utilized plant about 1,000 miles to combine it with another half-utilized plant producing a very similar kind of product. Because the products were launch vehicles, which are highly unforgiving of even tiny oversights, we planned the move in excruciating detail. Even so, we did experience an occasional "anomaly," to borrow a term from engineers. For example, when some of the factory workers from the old plant arrived at the new plant, they discovered that they did not have some of the more common machine settings they had been using. The reason: over the years, the workers had penciled those numbers on nearby posts supporting the factory's roof, and we had neglected to move the posts! In effecting change, a law of wing-walking always applies: Never let go of something until you have hold of something else. The good news is that we now have a string of 33 consecutive launches. The bad news is that you are no better than your last launch in this business. And that's true in most businesses.

VIII. Focus on the Customer

The *process* of change should be invisible to customers, but the *results* should be very apparent and very positive. Always underpromise and overproduce. Not doing so can be costly. My wife ordered some furniture through a retailer not long ago. Totally frustrated by a four-month delay in delivery, she finally called the manufacturer directly. The explanation? "Oh, we have just been through a merger." End of explanation. End of orders from my wife. Similarly, a defense-industry organization had held its annual three-day meeting at the same hotel for more than 50 years. One year, the hotel decided to reengineer its facilities all at once and told the organization to look elsewhere. Fortunately, the competitor across town *could* handle the meeting—and has been doing so ever since.

Even inside a company, almost every individual is a customer—a customer of coworkers. About 15 years ago at one of our electronics facilities in Orlando, Florida, the complacency bred of past success started to infect one of our manufacturing processes. Occasionally, parts were omitted from component kits prepared for assembly and inspection at another factory. Each missing part disrupted the assembly process and frustrated the workers assembling the products. I borrowed an idea from an automobile dealer in Dallas I had heard about. The dealer received few complaints from customers because he gave them the home telephone numbers of the mechanics who worked on their cars. I arranged for workers to include their names, work phone numbers, and self-addressed postcards in the kits they prepared. Complaints dropped precipitously.

Like the unicorn, the perfect restructuring effort exists only in the imagination.

IX. Be Decisive

Like the unicorn, the perfect restructuring effort exists only in the imagination. In reality, one is often faced with several equally unattractive options. When that happens, as President Truman once observed, "A leader has to lead."

When leaders are not decisive, very often few people are satisfied with the results. Consider the recent round of base closings suggested by the U.S. government's Base Closure and Realignment Commission (BRAC). The BRAC was established by Congress to take the politics out of the decision-making process of closing unnecessary defense installations. After months of study, debate, and deliberation, the BRAC made its recommendations—and the political potshots began. It would have been far preferable to leave the decision to those who would ultimately manage the facilities: the armed forces. The fact that such obvious solutions often prove politically untenable brings to mind the admonition of the late Louisiana senator Russell Long, who helped write much of the modern U.S. tax code: "Don't tax you, don't tax me. Tax that fellow behind the tree."

No decision will please everyone, but managers must make the tough decisions. If they do not, someone higher up in the organization will decide to replace them with others who will. As the nineteenth-century U.S. diplomat Edward John Phelps astutely noted, "The man who makes no mistakes does not usually make anything."

X. Create One Culture for One Company

Forging a culture from two existing ones means accepting the heretical notion that everything one group did in the past *wasn't* perfect and that everything the other group did *wasn't* flawed. Building a new culture means embracing the best of the best with an open mind.

All too often, however, the concept of culture thwarts instead of nurtures change. It is used as an excuse for not getting a difficult job done. Consider the story of a professional football player who was traded to a different team. In the first game with his new teammates, he repeatedly missed key blocks. When the coach finally called him to the sideline, the player said, "Coach, I'm having a big cultural problem out there." Ridiculous? Of course. Who would accept such an explanation? But then listen to a senior executive of a major aerospace company contemplating a major merger: "[Our company is] like the human body. It tends to reject transplants."

A critical challenge for managers leading a restructuring effort is inspiring individuals to work as a team. In fact, teamwork makes the difference for innumerable human endeavors and is absolutely essential for most business undertakings. In his rookie year with the Chicago Bulls, Stacey King inadvertently and somewhat humorously embodied the notions of team spirit and a sense of belonging. During one memorable game, King scored only 1 point while his teammate Michael Jordan scored 69. After the game, a reporter asked King for his reaction to the game. King said, "I'll always remember this as the night that Michael Jordan and I combined to score 70 points."

Soon after the 1993 merger of Martin Marietta and GE Aerospace, a videoconference was arranged between groups of employees from the two companies who were located in two different cities. During the conference, one group wore coats and ties or dresses, while the other group wore shirtsleeves, sweaters, and other casual clothing. At the next videoconference, those who had been in coats and ties now showed up in shirtsleeves, and vice versa. When the two groups saw each other,

Alfred P. Sloan, Jr., said it best: "Take my assets—but leave me my organization and in five years I'll have it all back."

laughter burst out on both sides. The experience did more for team building than anything management could have done. It demonstrated, once again, that given a reasonable chance, people will draw together for a common purpose. Managers must make clear what that purpose is.

XI. Remember That Your Real Assets Go Home at Night

Alfred P. Sloan, Jr., said it best: "Take my assets—but leave me my organization and in five years I'll have it all back." Neither machines nor bank accounts nor corporate policies will determine the success or failure of an effort to adapt to change. When all is said and done, successful change depends on individual people and their collective actions. By showing trust in and respect for all employees, managers can empower people to do their jobs to the very best of their ability. As Martin Marietta's former president, Tom Young, liked to observe, "No one shows up in the morning thinking, 'I guess I'll see how badly I can mess up today,' but an unenlightened management can put them in that frame of mind by 9 a.m." By cultivating and investing time in employees, managers strengthen the foundation of the entire enterprise.

For example, bringing customers in to speak to plant workers helps those workers appreciate the enormous importance of their jobs, especially when the customers are a pilot who flew one of our airplanes in the Persian Gulf War and an astronaut who will soon bet his life on one of our products. I try to demonstrate my faith in our employees' work in various ways, such as going on the first dive of a new nuclear submarine or, as in a recent trip to the South Pole, flying in an LC-130 aircraft that had been buried in ice for 16 years before being dug out and put back into service. Earlier this year, I even flew in one of our F-16 fighter aircraft.

Pay attention to symbols. For example, when we combined Lockheed's and Martin Marietta's headquarters in a building previously occupied by Martin Marietta, we moved everyone out and reassigned offices from scratch to avoid the impression that anyone had been bumped or that some people were more important than others. That action was critical from a social standpoint, and it is for that reason that we at Lockheed Martin try to treat acquisitions as mergers of equals. The attitude "we bought you" is a corporate cancer.

XII. Communicate, Communicate, Communicate

Despite the temptation to dispense only good news to the media, shareholders, customers, politicians, and employees, managers must be totally candid. As the great oracle Pogo once declared, "The certainty of misery is better than the misery of uncertainty." Unfortunately, in the case of the Lockheed-Martin Marietta merger, pain and unhappiness were inevitable as underutilized plants were closed and some employees were laid off. Our essential message was that bringing together the best practices of several distinct companies would make our new company far more competitive than any one of us would have been individually. Happily, that has indeed been true. So far, Lockheed Martin has enjoyed the greatest streak of new-business wins of which I am aware in our industry's history.

Right after the Lockheed Martin merger was consummated, Dan Tellep, who had been chairman of Lockheed, and I met with about 30,000 employees face-to-face in 62 meetings at individual plants and answered hundreds of questions. We encouraged brutally frank inquiries. "Why are you paid so much?" and "If you had just been transferred to this plant, would you rent or buy?" are only two examples of the questions we were asked. (Incidentally, my advice was to "lease with an option to buy.") We didn't sugarcoat any of our communications. We did our best to follow the advice of the great British author George Orwell, who wrote during the most difficult days of World War II, "The high sentiments always win in the end, the leaders who offer blood, toil, tears and sweat always get more out of their followers than those who offer safety and a good time. When it comes to the pinch, human beings are heroic." This certainly has been Lockheed Martin's experience.

T HIS DISCUSSION ENDS WHERE IT BEGAN—with the not terribly profound observation that virtually all businesses today find themselves in a fiercely competitive environment. The aerospace industry in particular has endured Darwinian pressures of an unprecedented magnitude, yet the industry now faces a future brighter than it has been in years. Had the industry not faced up to the challenges, it could easily have joined those who never reached the promising future that lay ahead.

When the Dow Jones Industrial Average recently marked its 100th anniversary, only one of the original companies had survived to join in the celebration: GE. A close reading of the *Fortune* 500 reveals an attrition rate of 7% per year. Even the 43 companies highlighted in Tom Peters and Bob Waterman's much acclaimed book of the 1980s, *In Search of Excellence*, have taken hits. A follow-up article in the November 5, 1984, issue of *Business Week* asserted that no fewer than 14 of the companies had already "lost their luster," at least in the sense that they had suffered serious profit erosion.

Apparently, excellence is a constantly moving target—a supposition Darwin himself may have had in mind. How can a business manager know that a battle for survival is imminent? Samuel Johnson wrote, "When a man knows he is to be hanged in a fortnight, it concentrates his mind wonderfully." In business, the "hanging" used to be the threat of bankruptcy—a threat that has become all too real for some high-profile companies.

In today's highly competitive marketplace, the hanging might be a poor earnings report, a product reliability problem, a technological breakthrough by a competitor, a lawsuit, or a political event halfway around the globe. The Information Age has narrowed the margin for error—a phenomenon such companies as Sears, Harley-Davidson, Kodak, IBM, and Chrysler all recognized in time to save themselves from the corporate graveyard.

Unfortunately, status-quo thinking is still common. As markets change, the established leaders are often among those most blinded by their past successes, not to mention their disproportionate stake in preserving the past. None of the companies that dominated the thriving ice-harvesting market in the nineteenth century converted to the refrigeration business. The Pony Express did not develop into a railroad. The producers of electromechanical calculators never made the techno-logical leap into electronic computers.

New expectations and new priorities are unsettling. And the fact that change is necessary in a global econ-omy based on free enterprise does not make it any more pleasant. But as former British prime minister Harold Wilson once observed, "He who rejects change is the architect of decay. The only human institution which rejects progress is the cemetery." Automotive executive Charles Kettering put it somewhat differently: "The world hates change, yet it is the only thing that has brought progress."

Business must be brilliant each and every day if a company is to survive. That is especially true in the high-tech world. As GE's Jack Welch has pointed out, to miss a generation in the computer market is to be out of business. The same is true in today's aerospace market. Witness McDonnell Douglas's recent loss in the next-generation fighter competition and the company's announcement less than a month later that it had agreed to be acquired by archrival Boeing. Technology-driven industries such as ours won't stand still and wait for individual companies to catch up. We have to reinvent ourselves continually. The bad news is that reengineering requires hard decisions. The good news is that success awaits organizations willing to make those decisions.

At Lockheed Martin, because of the enormous dedication of nearly 200,000 people, we now have at least a degree of control over our future. And the market has rewarded those efforts. Despite the near collapse of funding for our industry since the fall of the Berlin Wall, our company has shown a total annual return over five years of 29%—nearly twice the rate of increase of the S&P 500. What we do from this point on will, of course, depend on us. As Linus warned Charlie Brown, "There is no heavier burden than a great potential."

Originally published in May–June 1997
Reprint 97301

Successful Change Programs Begin with Results

ROBERT H. SCHAFFER AND
HARVEY A. THOMSON

Executive Summary

MOST CORPORATE IMPROVEMENT PROGRAMS have a negligible impact on operational and financial performance because management focuses on the activities, not the results. By initiating *activities-centered* programs, such as seven-step problem solving, statistical process control, and total quality management training, managers falsely assume that one day results will materialize. But because there is no explicit connection between action and outcome, improvements seldom do materialize. The authors argue for an alternative approach: *results-driven* improvement programs that focus on achievement specific, measurable operational improvements within a few months.

While both activity-centered and results-driven programs aim to strengthen fundamental corporate competitiveness, the approaches differ dramatically. Activity-centered programs rely on broad-based policies and are more concerned with time-consuming preparations than with measurable gains. Results-driven programs, on the other hand, rely on an incremental approach to change, building on what works and discarding what doesn't. As a result, successes come quickly, and managers build their skills and gain the support of their employees for future changes.

Because results-driven improvements require minimal investment, there is no excuse for postponing action. Indeed, there is always an abundance of underexploited capability and dissipated resources within the organization that management can tap into to get the program off the ground. The authors give a few pointers for how to get started: translate the long-term vision into doable but ambitious short-term goals: periodically review strategy, learning from both successes and failures; and institutionalize the changes that work and get rid of the rest.

THE PERFORMANCE IMPROVEMENT EFFORTS of many companies have as much impact on operational and financial results as a ceremonial rain dance has on the weather. While some companies constantly improve measurable performance, in many others, managers continue to dance round and round the campfire—exuding faith and dissipating energy.

This "rain dance" is the ardent pursuit of activities that sound good, look good, and allow managers to feel good—but in fact contribute little or nothing to bottom-line performance. These activities, many of which parade under the banner of "total quality" or "continuous improvement," typically advance a managerial philosophy or style such as interfunctional collaboration, middle management empowerment, or employee involvement. Some focus on measurement of performance such as competitive benchmarking, assessment of customer satisfaction, or statistical process controls. Still other activities aim at training employees in problem solving or other techniques.

Most improvement efforts have as much impact on company performance as a rain dance has on the weather.

Companies introduce these programs under the false assumption that if they carry out enough of the "right" improvement activities, actual performance improvements will inevitably materialize. At the heart of these programs, which we call "activity centered," is a fundamentally flawed logic that confuses ends with means, processes with outcomes. This logic is based on the belief that once managers benchmark their company's performance against competition, assess their customers' expectations, and train their employees in seven-step problem solving, sales will increase, inventory will shrink, and quality will improve. Staff experts and consultants tell management that it need not—in fact should not—focus directly on improving results because eventually results will take care of themselves.

The momentum for activity-centered programs continues to accelerate even though there is virtually no evidence to justify the flood of investment. Just the opposite: there is plenty of evidence that the rewards from these activities are illusory.

In 1988, for example, one of the largest U.S. financial institutions committed itself to a "total quality" program to improve operational performance and win customer loyalty. The company trained hundreds of people and communicated the program's intent to thousands more. At the end of two years of costly effort, the program's consultants summarized progress: "Forty-eight teams up and running. Two completed Quality Improvement Stories. Morale of employees regarding the process is very positive to date." They did not report any bottom-line performance improvements—because there were none.

The executive vice president of a large mineral-extracting corporation described the results of his company's three-year-old total quality program by stating, "We have accomplished about 50% of our training goals and about 50% of our employee participation goals but only about 5% of our results goals." And he considered those results meritorious.

These are not isolated examples. In a 1991 survey of more than 300 electronics companies, sponsored by the American Electronics Association, 73% of the companies reported having a total quality program under way; but of these, 63% had failed to improve quality defects by even as much as 10%. We believe this survey understates the magnitude of the failure of activity-centered programs not only in the quality-conscious electronics industry but across all businesses.

These signs suggest a tragedy in the making: pursuing the present course, companies will not achieve significant progress in their overall competitiveness. They will continue to spend vast resources on a variety of activities, only to watch cynicism grow in the ranks. And eventually, management will discard many potentially useful improvement processes because it expected the impossible of them and came up empty-handed.

If activity-centered programs have yielded such paltry returns on the investment, why are so many companies continuing to pour money and energy into them? For the same reason that previous generations of management invested in zero-based budgeting, Theory Z, and quality circles. Years of frustrating attempts to keep pace with fast-moving competitors make managers prey to almost any plausible approach. And the fact that hundreds of membership associations, professional societies, and consulting firms all promote activity-centered processes lends them an aura of popularity and legitimacy. As a consequence, many senior managers have become convinced that all of these preparatory activities really will pay off some day and that there isn't a viable alternative.

They are wrong on both counts. Any payoffs from the infusion of activities will be meager at best. And there is in fact an alternative: results-driven improvement processes that focus on achieving specific, measurable operational improvements within a few months. This means increased yields, reduced delivery time, increased inventory turns, improved customer satisfaction, reduced product development time. With results-driven improvements, a company introduces only those innovations in management methods and business processes that can help achieve specific goals. (See "Comparing Improvement Efforts.")

An automotive-parts plant, whose customers were turning away from it because of poor quality and late deliveries, illustrates the difference between the two approaches. To solve the company's problems, management launched weekly employee-involvement team meetings focused on improving quality. By the end of six months, the teams had generated hundreds of suggestions and abundant goodwill in the plant but virtually no improvement in quality or delivery.

Comparing Improvement Efforts

While activity-centered programs and results-driven programs share some common methodologies for initiating change, they differ in very dramatic ways.

Results-Driven Programs 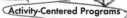 **Activity-Centered Programs**

1. The improvement effort is defined mainly in long-term, global terms. ("We are going to be viewed as number one in quality in our industry.")

2. Management takes action steps because they are "correct" and fit the program's philosophy. ("I want every manager in the division involved in an action.")

3. The program's champion(s) counsels patience and fortitude. ("Don't be looking for results this year or next year. This is a long-term process, not a quick fix.")

4. Staff experts and consultants indoctrinate everyone into the mystique and vocabulary of the program. ("It will be a Tower of Babel if we try to work on these problems before everyone, managers and employees alike, has been through the quality training and has a common vocabulary and a common tool kit.")

5. Staff experts and consultants urge managers and employees to have faith in the approach and to support it. ("True employee involvement will take a lot of time and a lot of effort, and though it may be a real struggle for managers, they need to understand that it is essential to become a total quality company.")

6. The process requires management to make big investments up front—before results have been demonstrated. ("During the first year, we expect to concentrate on awareness building and skill training. Then, while managers begin to diagnose problems and opportunities in their areas, a consultant will be surveying all of our customers to get their views on the 14 critical dimensions of service. And then . . .")

1. There are measurable short-term performance improvement goals, even though the effort is a long-term, sustaining one. ("Within 60 days, we will be paying 95% of claims within 10 days.")

2. Management takes action steps because they appear to lead directly toward some improved results. ("Let's put together a small group to work with you to solve this machine downtime problem.")

3. The mood is one of impatience. Management wants to see results now, even though the change process is a long-term commitment. ("If we can't eliminate at least half of the cost disadvantage within the next three months, we should consider closing the plant.")

4. Staff experts and consultants help managers achieve results. ("We could probably work up a way to measure customer attitudes on delivery service within a week or two so that you can start improving it.")

5. Managers and employees are encouraged to make certain for themselves that the approach actually yields results. ("Why don't you send a few of your people to the quality course to test out whether it really helps them achieve their improvement goals in the next month or two.")

6. Relatively little investment is needed to get the process started; conviction builds as results materialize. ("Let's see if this approach can help us increase sales of high-end products in a couple of branches. If it does, we can take the method to the other branches.")

In a switch to a results-driven approach, management concentrated on one production line. The plant superintendent asked the manager of that line to work with his employees and with plant engineering to reduce by 30% the frequency of their most prevalent defect within two months. This sharply focused goal was reached on time. The manager and his team next agreed to cut the occurrence of that same defect by an additional 50%. They also broadened the effort to encompass other kinds of defects on the line. Plant management later extended the process to other production lines, and within about four months the plant's scrap rate was within budgeted limits.

Both activity-centered and results-driven strategies aim to strengthen fundamental corporate competitiveness. But as the automotive-parts plant illustrates, the approaches differ dramatically. The activities path is littered with the remains of endless preparatory investments that failed to yield the desired outcomes. The results-driven path stakes out specific targets and matches resources, tools, and action plans to the requirements of reaching those targets. As a consequence, managers know what they are trying to achieve, how and when it should be done, and how it can be evaluated.

The Activity-Centered Fallacy

There are six reasons why the cards are stacked against activity-centered improvement programs:

1. *Not Keyed to Specific Results.* In activity-centered programs, managers reform the way they work with each other and with employees; they train people; they develop new measurement schemes; they increase employee

awareness of customer attitudes, quality, and more. The expectation is that these steps will lead to better business performance. But managers rarely make explicit how the activity is supposed to lead to the result.

Seeking to improve quality, senior management at a large telecommunications equipment corporation sent a number of unit managers to quality training workshops. When they returned, the unit heads ordered orientation sessions for middle management. They also selected and trained facilitators who, in turn, trained hundreds of supervisors and operators in statistical process control. But senior management never specified which performance parameters it wanted to improve—costs, reject rates, delivery timeliness. During the following year, some units improved performance along some dimensions, other units improved along others, and still other units saw no improvement at all. There was no way for management to assess whether there was any connection between the investment in training and specific, tangible results.

One company identified so many activities in so many places, it required a complex chart just to describe them.

2. *Too Large Scale and Diffused.* The difficulty of connecting activities to the bottom line is complicated by the fact that most companies choose to launch a vast array of activities simultaneously across the entire organization. This is like researching a cure for a disease by giving a group of patients ten different new drugs at the same time.

In one case, a large international manufacturer identified almost 50 different activities that it wanted built into its total quality effort. The company's list involved so many programs introduced in so many places that just to describe them all required a complex chart. Once top managers had made the investment and the public commitment, however, they "proved" their wisdom by crediting the programs for virtually any competitive gain the company made. But in fact, no one knew for sure which, if any, of the 50 activities were actually working.

3. *Results Is a Four-Letter Word.* When activity-centered programs fail to produce improvement in financial and operational performance, managers seldom complain lest they be accused of preoccupation with the short term at the expense of the long term—the very sin that has supposedly caused companies to defer investment in capital and human resources and thus to lose their competitive edge. It is a brave manager who will insist on seeing a demonstrable link between the proposed investment and tangible payoffs in the short term.

When one company had little to show for the millions of dollars it invested in improvement activities, the chief operations officer rationalized, "You can't expect to overturn 50 years of culture in just a couple of years." And he urged his management team to persevere in its pursuit of the activities.

He is not alone in his faith that, given enough time, activity-centered efforts will pay off. The company cited above, with almost 50 improvement activities going at once, published with pride its program's timetable calling for three years of preparations and reformations, with major results expected only in the fourth year. And at a large electronics company, the manual explaining its management-empowerment process warned that implementation could be "painful" and that management should not expect to see results for a "long time."

4. *Delusional Measurements.* Having conveyed the false message that activities will inevitably produce results, the activities promoters compound the crime by

"Success" at one company consisted of getting 100% of each unit's employees to attend a quality training program.

equating measures of activities with actual improvements in performance. Companies proclaim their quality programs with the same pride with which they would proclaim real performance improvements—ignoring or perhaps even unaware of the significance of the difference.

In a leading U.S. corporation, we found that a group of quality facilitators could not enumerate the critical business goals of their units. Surprised, we asked how they could possibly assess whether or not they were successful. Their answer: success consisted of getting 100% of each unit's managers and employees to attend the prescribed quality training—a centerpiece of the corporation's total quality program.

The Malcolm Baldrige National Quality Award encourages such practices by devoting only 180 points out of a possible 1,000 points to quality results. The award gives high marks to companies that demonstrate outstanding quality processes without always demanding that the current products and services be equally outstanding.

5. *Staff- and Consultant-Driven.* The focus on activities as ends in themselves is exacerbated by the fact that improvement programs are usually designed by staff specialists, external consultants, or other experts, rather than by operating managers. In many cases, managers seek this outside help because they have exhausted their

own ideas about improvement. So when staff experts and improvement gurus show up with their evangelistic enthusiasm and bright promises of total quality and continuous improvement, asking only for faith and funds, managers greet them with open arms.

But the capability of most of these improvement experts is limited to installing discrete, often generic packages of activities that are rarely aimed directly at specific results. They design training courses; they launch self-directed teams; they create new quality-measurement systems; they organize campaigns to win the Baldrige Award. Senior managers plunge whole-heartedly into these activities, relieving themselves, momentarily at least, of the burden of actually having to improve performance.

The automotive-parts plant described earlier illustrates the pattern. Senior managers had become very frustrated after a number of technical solutions failed to cure the plant's ills. When a staff group then asserted that employee involvement could produce results, management quickly accepted the staff group's suggestion to initiate employee-involvement team meetings—meetings that failed to deliver results.

The futility of expecting staff-driven programs to yield performance improvement was highlighted in a study conducted by a Harvard Business School team headed by Michael Beer. It analyzed a number of large-scale corporate change programs, some of which had succeeded, others of which had failed. The study found that company wide change programs installed by staff groups did not lead to successful transformation. As the authors colorfully put it, "Wave after wave of programs rolled across the landscape with little positive impact."[1]

6. *Bias to Orthodoxy, Not Empiricism.* Because of the absence of clear-cut beginnings and ends and an inability to link cause and effect, there is virtually no opportunity in activity-centered improvement programs to learn useful lessons and apply them to future programs. Instead, as in any approach based on faith rather than evidence, the advocates—convinced they already know all the answers—merely urge more dedication to the "right" steps.

One manufacturing company, for example, launched almost 100 quality improvement teams as a way to "get people involved." These teams produced scores of recommendations for process changes. The result was stacks of work orders piling up in maintenance, production engineering, and systems departments—more than any of these groups were capable of responding to. Senior managers, however, believed the outpouring of suggestions reinforced their original conviction that participation would succeed. Ignoring mounting evidence that the process was actually counterproductive, they determined to get even more teams established.

Results-Driven Transformation

In stark contrast to activity-centered programs, results-driven improvements bypass lengthy preparation rituals and aim at accomplishing measurable gains rapidly. Consider the case of the Morgan Bank. When told that his units would have to compete on an equal footing with outside vendors, the senior vice president of the bank's administrative services (responsible for 20 service functions including printing, food services, and purchasing) realized that the keys to survival were better service and lower costs. To launch a response, he asked the head of each of the service functions to select one or two service-improvement goals that were important to internal "customers" and could be achieved quickly. Unit heads participated in several workshops and worked with consultants but always maintained a clear focus on launching the improvement processes that would enable them to achieve their goals.

In the bank's microfilm department, for example, the first goal was to meet consistently a 24-hour turnaround deadline for the work of a stock-transfer department. The microfilm department had frequently missed this deadline, sometimes by several days. The three shift supervisors and their manager laid out a five-week plan to accomplish the goal. They introduced a number of work-process innovations, each selected on the basis of its capacity to help achieve the 24-hour turnaround goal, and tracked performance improvements daily.

Results-driven programs bypass lengthy preparations and aim for quick, measurable gains within a few months.

This project, together with similar results-driven projects simultaneously carried out in the other 19 units, yielded significant service improvements and several million dollars of cost savings within the first year of the initiative—just about the time it usually takes to design the training programs and get all employees trained in a typical activity-centered effort. The experience of the Morgan Bank illustrates four key benefits of a results-driven approach that activity-centered programs generally miss:

1. *Companies introduce managerial and process innovations only as they are needed.* Results-driven projects require managers to prioritize carefully the innovations they want to employ to achieve targeted goals. Managers

introduce modifications in management style, work
methods, goal setting, information systems, and customer relationships in a just-in-time mode when the
change appears capable of speeding progress toward
measurable goals. Contrast this with activity-centered
programs, where all employees may be ritualistically
sent off for training because it is the "right" thing to do.

In the Morgan Bank's microfilm department project,
the three shift supervisors worked together as a unified
team—not to enhance teamwork but to figure out how
to reduce customer delivery time. For the first time ever,
they jointly created a detailed improvement work plan
and week-by-week subgoals. They posted this work plan
next to a chart showing daily performance. Employees
on all three shifts actively participated in the project,
offering suggestions for process changes, receiving
essential training that was immediately applied, and taking responsibility for implementation.

Thus instead of making massive investments to
infuse the organization with a hodgepodge of improvement activities, the microfilm department and each of
the other administrative services introduced innovations
incrementally, in support of specific performance goals.

2. *Empirical testing reveals what works.* Because management introduces each managerial and process innovation sequentially and links them to short-term goals, it
can discover fairly quickly the extent to which each
approach yields results. In the Morgan Bank's microfilm
department, for example, the creation of a detailed
improvement work plan and week-by-week subgoals—
which were introduced during the first two weeks of the
program—enabled management to assess accurately
and quickly the impact of its actions in meeting the 24-
hour turnaround goal.

New procedures for communicating between shifts allowed management to anticipate workload peaks and to reassign personnel from one shift to another. That innovation contributed to meeting deadlines. A new numbering system to identify the containers of work from different departments did not contribute, and management quickly abandoned the innovation. By constantly assessing how each improvement step contributed to meeting deadlines, management made performance improvement less an act of faith and more an act of rational decision making based on evidence.

3. *Frequent reinforcement energizes the improvement process.* There is no motivator more powerful than frequent successes. By replacing large-scale, amorphous improvement objectives with short-term, incremental projects that quickly yield tangible results, managers and employees can enjoy the psychological fruits of success. Demonstrating to themselves their capacity to succeed not only provides necessary reinforcement but also builds management's confidence and skill for continued incremental improvements.

The manager of the bank's microfilm department, for example, had never had the experience of leading a significant upgrading of performance. It was not easy for her to launch the process in the face of employee skepticism. Within a few weeks, however, when the chart on the wall showed the number of missed deadlines going down, everyone took pleasure in seeing it, and work went forward with renewed vigor. The manager's confidence grew and so did employee support for the subsequent changes she implemented.

In another example, a division of Motorola wanted to accelerate new product development. To get started, a management team selected two much-delayed mobile

two-way radios and focused on bringing these products
to the market within 90 days. For each product, the
team created a unified, multifunction work plan;
appointed a single manager to oversee the entire development process as the product moved from department
to department; and designated an interfunctional team
to monitor progress. With these and other innovations,
both radios were launched on time. This success encouraged management to extend the innovations to other
new product projects and eventually to the entire product development process.

4. *Management creates a continuous learning process
by building on the lessons of previous phases in designing
the next phase of the program.* Both activity-centered
and results-driven programs are ultimately aimed at
producing fundamental shifts in the performance of the
organization. But unlike activity-centered programs that
focus on sweeping cultural changes, large-scale training
programs, and massive process innovation, results-
driven programs begin by identifying the most urgently
needed performance improvements and carving off
incremental goals to achieve quickly.

By using each incremental project as a testing ground
for new ways of managing, measuring, and organizing
for results, management gradually creates a foundation
of experience on which to build an organization-wide
performance improvement. Once the manager of Morgan's microfilm department succeeded in meeting the
24-hour turnaround goal for one internal customer
department, she extended the process to other customer
departments.

In each of the other 19 service units, the same expansion was taking place. Unit managers shared their
experiences in formal review conferences so that every-

one could benefit from the best practices. Within six months, every manager and supervisor in administrative services was actively leading one or more improvement projects. From a base of real results, managers were able to encourage a continuous improvement process to spread, and they introduced dozens of managerial innovations in the course of achieving sizable performance gains.

Putting the Ideas into Practice

Taking advantage of the power of results-driven improvements calls for a subtle but profound shift in mind-set: management begins by identifying the performance improvements that are most urgently needed and then, instead of studying and preparing and gearing up and delaying, sets about at once to achieve some measurable progress in a short time.

The Eddystone Generating Station of Philadelphia Electric, once the world's most efficient fossil-fuel plant, illustrates the successful shift from activity-centered to results-driven improvement. As Eddystone approached its thirtieth anniversary, its thermal efficiency—the amount of electricity produced from each ton of coal burned—had declined significantly. The problem was serious enough that top management was beginning to question the plant's continued operation.

The station's engineers had initiated many corrective actions, including installing a state-of-the-art computerized system to monitor furnace efficiency, upgrading plant equipment and materials, and developing written procedures for helping operating staff run the plant more efficiently. But because the innovations were not built into the day-to-day operating routine of the plant, thermal efficiency tended to deteriorate when the engineers turned their attention elsewhere.

In September 1990, the superintendent of operations decided to take a results-driven approach to improve thermal efficiency. He and his management team committed to achieve a specific incremental improvement of thermal efficiency worth about $500,000 annually—without any additional plant investment. To get started, they identified a few improvements that they could accomplish within three months and established teams to tackle each one.

A five-person team of operators and maintenance employees and one supervisor took responsibility for reducing steam loss from hundreds of steam valves throughout the plant. The team members started by eliminating all the leaks in one area of the plant. Then they moved on to other areas. In the process, they invented improvements in valve-packing practices and devised new methods for reporting leaks.

Another employee team was assigned the task of reducing heat that escaped through openings in the huge furnaces. For its first subproject, the group ensured that all 96 inspection doors on the furnace walls were operable and were closed when not in use. Still

At a power station, two tons of coal dumped in the manager's parking space dramatized poor thermal efficiency.

another team, this one committed to reducing the amount of unburned carbon that passed through the furnace, began by improving the operating effectiveness of the station's coal-pulverizer mills in order to improve the carbon burn rate.

Management charged each of these cross-functional teams not merely with studying and recommending but also with producing measurable results in a methodical, step-by-step fashion. A steering committee of station managers met every two weeks to review progress and help overcome obstacles. A variety of communication mechanisms built awareness of the project and its progress. For example, to launch the process, the steering committee piled two tons of coal in the station manager's parking space to dramatize the hourly cost of poor thermal efficiency. In a series of "town meetings" with all employees, managers explained the reason for the effort and how it would work. Newsletters reviewed progress on the projects—including the savings realized—and credited employees who had contributed to the effort.

As each team reached its goal, the steering committee, in consultation with supervisors and employees, identified the next series of performance improvement goals, such as the reduction of the plant's own energy consumption, and commissioned a number of teams and individuals to implement a new round of projects. By the end of the first year, efficiency improvements were saving the company over $1 million a year, double the original goal.

Beyond the monetary gains—gains achieved with negligible investment—Eddystone's organizational structure began to change in profound ways. What had been a hierarchical, tradition-bound organization became more flexible and open to change. Setting and achieving ambitious short-term goals became part of the plant's regular routine as managers pushed decisions further and further down into the organization. Eventually, the station manager disbanded the steering

committee, and now everyone who manages improvement projects reports directly to the senior management team.

Eddystone managers and workers at all levels continue to experiment and have invented a number of
highly creative efficiency-improving processes. A change
so profound could never have happened by sending all
employees to team training classes and then telling
them, "Now you are empowered; go to it."

In the course of accomplishing its results, Eddystone
management introduced many of the techniques that
promoters of activity-centered programs insist must be
drilled into the organization for months or years before
gains can be expected: employees received training in
various analytical techniques; team-building exercises
helped teams achieve their goals more quickly; teams
introduced new performance measurements as they
were needed; and managers analyzed and redesigned
work processes. But unlike activity-centered programs,
the results-driven work teams introduced innovations
only if they could contribute to the realization of short-
term goals. They did not inject innovations wholesale in
the hope that they would somehow generate better
results. There was never any doubt that responsibility
for results was in the hands of accountable managers.

Philadelphia Electric—and many other companies as
well—launched its results-driven improvement process
with a few modest pilot projects. Companies that want
to launch large-scale change, however, can employ a
results-driven approach across a broad front. In 1988,
chairman John F. Welch, Jr. launched General Electric's
"Work-Out" process across the entire corporation. The
purpose was to overcome bureaucracy and eliminate
business procedures that interfered with customer

responsiveness. The response of GE's $3 billion Lighting Business illustrates how such a large-scale improvement process can follow a results-driven pathway.

Working sessions attended by a large cross-section of Lighting employees, a key feature of Work-Out, identified a number of "quick wins" in target areas. These were initiatives that employees could take right away to generate measurable improvement in a short time. To speed new product development, for example, Work-Out participants recommended that five separate functional review sessions be combined into one, a suggestion that was eagerly adopted. To get products to customers more quickly, a team tested the idea of working with customers and a trucking company to schedule, in advance, regular delivery days for certain customers. The results of the initial pilot were so successful that GE Lighting has extended the scheduling system to hundreds of customers.

Another team worked to reduce the breakage of fragile products during shipment—costly both in direct dollars and in customer dissatisfaction. Sub-teams, created to investigate package design and shipping-pallet construction, followed sample shipments from beginning to end and asked customers for their ideas. Within weeks, the team members had enough information to shift to remedial action. They tried many innovations in the packaging design; they modified work processes in high-risk areas; they reduced the number of times each product is handled; they collaborated with their shippers, suppliers, and customers. The payoff was a significant reduction in breakage within a few months.

The Lighting Business has launched dozens of such results-oriented projects quickly—and as each project achieves results, management has launched additional projects and has even extended the process to its European operations.

Opportunities for Change

There is no reason for senior-level managers to acquiesce when their people plead that they are already accomplishing just about all that can be accomplished or that factors beyond their control—company policy, missing technology, or lack of resources—are blocking accelerated performance improvement. Such self-limiting ideas are universal. Instead, management needs to recognize that there is an abundance of both under-exploited capability and dissipated resources in the organization.

This orientation frees managers to set about translating potential into results and to avoid the cul-de-sac of fixing up and reforming the organization in preparation for future progress. Here is how management can get started in results-driven programs:

1. *Ask each unit to set and achieve a few ambitious short-term performance goals.* There is no organization where management could not start to improve performance quickly with the resources at hand—even in the face of attitudinal and skill deficiencies, personnel and other resource limitations, unstable market conditions, and every other conceivable obstacle. To begin with, managers can ask unit heads to commit to achieve in a short time some improvement targets, such as faster turnaround time in responding to customers, lower costs, increased sales, or improved cash flow. They should also be asked to test some managerial, process, or technical innovations that can help them reach their goals.

2. *Periodically review progress, capture the essential learning, and reformulate strategy.* Results-driven improvement is an empirical process in which managers use the experience of each phase as data for shaping the next phase. In scheduled work sessions, senior management should review and evaluate progress on the current array of results-focused projects and learn what is and what isn't working.

Fresh insights flood in from these early experiments: how rapidly project teams can make gains; what kind of support they need; what changes in work methods they can implement quickly; what kinds of obstacles need to be addressed at higher levels in the organization. Managers and employees develop confidence in their capacity to get things done and to challenge and overturn obsolete practices.

Armed with this learning, senior management can refine strategies and timetables and, in consultation with their people, can carve out the next round of business goals. The cycle repeats and expands as confidence and momentum grow.

3. *Institutionalize the changes that work—and discard the rest.* As management gains experience, it can take steps to institutionalize the practices and technologies that contribute most to performance improvement and build those into the infrastructure of the company. In Motorola's Mobile Division, for example, in its new product development project, a single manager was assigned responsibility for moving each new product from engineering to production and to delivery, as opposed to having this responsibility handed off from function to function. This worked so well it became standard practice.

Such change can also take place at the policy level. A petroleum company, for example, experimented with incentive compensation in two sales districts. When the trials produced higher sales growth, senior management decided to install throughout the marketing function a performance-based compensation plan that reflected what it had learned in the experiments. In this way, a company can gradually build successful innovations into its operations and discard unsuccessful ones before they do much harm.

4. *Create the context and identify the crucial business challenges.* Senior management must establish the broader framework to guide continuing performance improvement in the form of strategic directions for the business and a "vision" of how it will operate in the future. A creative vision can be a source of inspiration and motivation for managers and employees who are being asked to help bring about change. But no matter how imaginative the vision might be, for it to contribute to accelerated progress, managers must translate it into sharp and compelling expectations for short-term performance achievements. At Philadelphia Electric, for example, the Eddystone improvement work responded to top management's insistent call for performance improvement and cost reduction.

A results-driven improvement process does not relieve senior management of the responsibility to make the difficult strategic decisions necessary for the company's survival and prosperity. General Electric's Work-Out process augmented but could never substitute for Jack Welch's dramatic restructuring and downsizing moves. By marrying long-term strategic objectives with short-term improvement projects, however, management can translate strategic direction into reality and resist the temptation to inculcate the rain dance of activity-centered programs.

Notes

1. See Michael Beer, Russell A. Eisenstat, and Bert Spector, "Why Change Programs Don't Produce Change," *Harvard Business Review,* November–December 1990, p. 158.

Originally published in January–February 1992
Reprint 92108

About the Contributors

ANTHONY ATHOS held the Jesse Isidor Chair of Business Administration at Harvard Business School until 1982, when he resigned to devote himself to coaching senior executives full-time. He is perhaps best known as an outstanding teacher-lecturer and is the coauthor with Richard Pascale of *The Art of Japanese Management.*

NORMAN R. AUGUSTINE served as chairman and CEO of Martin Marietta for eight years until it became part of Lockheed Martin, where he also served as chairman and CEO. He is a member of the board of directors of Phillips Petroleum, Procter & Gamble, and Black & Decker, and is chairman of the American Red Cross. Currently he is a faculty member of Princeton University in the School of Engineering and Applied Science. He was recently awarded the National Medal of Technology by the president of the United States.

JAMES C. COLLINS is coauthor of *Built to Last: Successful Habits of Visionary Companies.* He operates a management research and teaching laboratory in Boulder, Colorado.

JEANIE DANIEL DUCK joined The Boston Consulting Group (BCG) as a vice president in 1988. She is presently based in the Atlanta office and is an active contributor to BCG's worldwide Organizational Practice Group. Her focus is on the overall architecture of organizational transformation and all the elements that entails—designing, coordinating, and managing. She is the author of several articles and has taught at both the University of Alabama, Birmingham, and at Pratt Institute in New York where she received her Master of Science degree.

TRACY GOSS is a noted author, lecturer, and consultant. She is the originator of Executive Re-Invention and author of *The Last Word on Power: Executive Re-Invention for Leaders Who Must Make the Impossible Happen.* As president of Goss Reid Associates, a management consulting firm based in Austin, Texas, she consults with CEOs and senior executives leading corporate re-invention in major national and international companies. She recently co-founded The Center for Executive Re-Invention.

JOHN P. KOTTER is Konosuke Matsushita Professor of Leadership at the Harvard Business School, where he teaches in both MBA and executive programs, and is a frequent speaker at top management meetings around the world. He is the author of several best-selling business books, including his most recent book, *Leading Change* (HBS Press, 1996). Professor Kotter was the recipient of the Exxon Award for Innovation in Graduate Business School Curriculum Design and the Johnson, Smith & Knisely Award for New Perspectives in Business Leadership.

ROGER MARTIN is a director of Monitor Company, a global strategy consulting firm that works with clients to ensure that they take the necessary actions to build and sustain competitive advantage. His current practice focuses on building the capabilities of management teams to work productively together to resolve strategic challenges. Using both strategic analysis and organizational learning disciplines he has created a new process to help teams make significant, strategic choices in an efficient and consensus-producing manner. He is currently working on his first book, *The Responsibility Virus*, which focuses on correctly assigning duties and tasks in organizations.

RICHARD PASCALE is an associate fellow of Oxford University and a visiting scholar of the Santa Fe Institute. He was a member of the faculty at Stanford's Graduate School of Business for twenty years. He is a leading business consultant worldwide, a best-selling author, and a respected scholar. Dr. Pascale is co-author of *The Art of Japanese Management*, a *New York Times* best-seller, and author of *Managing on the Edge*. His seminal *Harvard Business Review* article, "Zen and the Art of Management," won a McKinsey Award. He has worked closely with two dozen CEOs and top management teams of *Fortune* 500 firms engaged in organizational transformation.

JERRY I. PORRAS is the Lane Professor of Organizational Behavior and Change at the Graduate School of Business, Stanford University. He is the director of Stanford's executive program in leading and managing change and teaches MBA courses in visionary companies, leadership, organizational development, and interpersonal dynamics. Dr. Porras is the author of *Stream Analysis: A Powerful New Way to Diagnose and Manage Organizational Change*, and co-author of *Built to Last: Successful Habits of Visionary Companies*, which has been translated into thirteen languages. He has served on the editorial boards of the *Academy of Management Journal*, *Academy of Management Review*, *Journal of Applied Behavioral Science*, *Business Review*, and *Journal of Organizational Change Management*.

ROBERT H. SCHAFFER founded Robert H. Schaffer & Associates and has been its head for more than thirty years. He is the originator of the firm's unique results-driven change management process, described in his 1988 book, *The Break-through Strategy*. In addition to "Successful Change Programs Begin with Results," he has written four other *Harvard Business Review* articles, including "Demand Better Results—and Get Them," which became an HBR "classic." His latest book, *High-Impact Consulting: How Clients and Consultants Can Leverage Rapid Results into Long-Term Gains*, was published in 1997.

PAUL STREBEL is the director of the International Institute for Management Development's program on leading corporate change. He is an expert on strategic change management, especially the anticipation of industry breakpoints and the design of new compacts to support ongoing change. Mr. Strebel is the author of *Breakpoints: How Managers Exploit Radical Business Change* (HBS Press, 1992) and *New Compacts: For Frontline Commitment to Ongoing Change*, which is due to be released in 1998. He is a consultant on change management to multinational companies and sits on the boards of several family-owned companies.

HARVEY A. THOMSON is a principal at Robert H. Schaffer & Associates. He manages the firm's Canadian operations and assists senior managers in the public and private sectors to plan and carry out results-oriented improvement and change programs. Mr. Thomson was previously a professor of management at McGill University.

Index

Knowledge is Power.
(So don't forget to recharge.)

For e-mail updates on powerful new business ideas and management issues, sign up for the *Harvard Business Review* listserv at **www.hbsp.harvard.edu.**

For ideas any time keep the Harvard Business School Publishing Web page in mind.

○ Access more than 7,500 articles, books, case studies, videos and CD-ROMs by leaders in management practice.
○ Search by author, key word, and more.
○ Order on-line and download *Harvard Business Review* articles any time.

Visit **www.hbsp.harvard.edu**, or call **(800) 668-6780** or **(617) 496-1449.**

Harvard Business School Publishing
The power of ideas at work.